LOANS & GRANTS FROM UNCLE SAM

Am I Eligible and for How Much?

EIGHTEENTH EDITION
ANNA LEIDER

OCTAMERON
ASSOCIATES

Address editorial correspondence to:

Octameron Associates
PO Box 2748
Alexandria, VA 22301
703/836-5480 (voice)
703/836-5650 (fax)

octameron@aol.com (e-mail)
www.octameron.com

ISBN 1-57509-141-0

PRINTED IN THE UNITED STATES OF AMERICA

CONTENTS

....

CHAPTER 1

∎∎∎∎∎∎∎∎∎∎∎∎∎∎∎∎∎∎∎∎

APPLYING FOR
FEDERAL STUDENT AID

Leider's Law: Any reduction in the funding of governmental social programs will lead to an increase in the complexity of administering the remaining dollars. From this it follows that the number of program administrators will increase in inverse proportion to the number of program beneficiaries.

The Purpose of This Guide

Right now, federal student aid programs are managed so that Uncle Sam holds all the cards. The purpose of this guide is to deal you a hand with at least one ace, so you can play more effectively; maybe even win the first round. Our primary goal is to help you overcome the program's biggest flaw: its disastrous timing. We want you to be able to assess your eligibility for federal aid when you start choosing colleges.

	Oct	Nov	Dec	Jan	Feb	Mar	Apr	May

College Selection ▬▬▬▬▬▬▬▬▬▬

College Acceptance ▬▬▬▬▬▬▬▬▬▬

Federal Aid Applications ▬▬▬▬▬▬▬▬▬

Financial Aid Award Letter ▬▬▬▬▬▬▬▬

As you can see from the chart above, you may not learn whether you're eligible for aid until after you've picked and been accepted by the college(s) of your choice. Should you learn that Uncle won't help, or will help with fewer dollars than expected, your carefully laid plans may no longer possible. You may have to start over, and with little time to spare. We don't want this to happen.

But even this chart is theoretical. In fact, you may not know the composition of your aid package until much later. And even then, mid-year rescission bills can shrink the grant you'd already been promised while mid-year rule "clarifications" can make you suddenly ineligible for federal funds altogether. Even if the rules don't change, Uncle Sam can be so late getting information to aid administrators, they aren't sure which end is up.

Eligibility for Federal Student Aid

You can receive federal student aid if:

1. You are a US citizen or national; a US permanent resident; or an eligible non-citizen (e.g., a refugee or a person granted asylum).
2. You are enrolled in an "eligible" program at an "eligible" school. Students working toward associate, bachelor or graduate degrees need not worry much about what makes a program "eligible." Students looking at correspondence schools or proprietary schools should inquire about the school's status before sending off tuition deposits.
3. You have certified that you are not in default on any federal student loans (unless you've made satisfactory repayment arrangements), nor have you borrowed in excess of the allowable limits. This statement appears on the aid application.
4. You are registered with Selective Service (males age 18 through 25).
5. You promise that all money received will be used for educational expenses at XYZ college. This statement appears on the aid application.
6. You have a HS diploma or its equivalent, or have met other basic standards as established by your state (and approved by Uncle Sam). Home-schooled students without the equivalent of a high school diploma are eligible for federal student aid if they have completed a secondary school education in a state-recognized home school setting.
7. You are making satisfactory progress in your course of study.
8. You have a valid Social Security Number.
9. You show you have need (to qualify for any need-based program).

Special Eligibility Situations

Study Abroad. You are eligible for aid if the program is approved for credit by your school (assuming you are attending an "eligible" school). Furthermore, there must be a contractual agreement between the home institution and the international school.

Distance Education. You can receive federal aid if the course is part of an accredited program.

Jail. Students incarcerated in federal or state institutions are not eligible for federal student loans or Pell grants; they may, however, receive Supplemental Educational Opportunity Grants and Federal Work-Study.

Students incarcerated in local institutions are not eligible for federal student loans, however they may receive Pells, SEOGs, and Work-Study.

Demonstrating Need

Demonstrating need for federal student aid begins with a formula applied to the information you submit on your aid application. The formula has numerous elements, some of which change annually.

Visualize the formula as a long row of machines that pound, grind, stretch and squeeze. Your financial information is fed to these machines. After it has been pounded, ground, stretched and squeezed, it emerges as your **Expected Family Contribution (EFC)**. You can use the appendices to estimate your family's EFC.

If your EFC is less than your college's cost of attendance, you are eligible for federal need-based aid (Perkins and Stafford Loans, Work-Study and Supplemental Educational Opportunity Grants). If your EFC is less than about $5,200, you'll be eligible for a Pell Grant as well.

Dependent vs. Independent Student

The financial aid process classifies students by dependency status:

Dependent students are at least partially dependent on their parents for support. The income and assets of both student and parent are used to determine the amount a family must contribute to college costs.

Independent students are not dependent on their parents for support. Only their own income and assets (and those of any spouse) are evaluated to determine contribution to college costs. Establishing independence usually gives you an advantage: By not having to include parental income and assets, your expected contribution will most likely be lower and that will result in more student aid.

To be considered independent under federal regulations, a student must meet one of the following conditions:

1. Be 24 years of age by December 31 of the award year (for example, December 31, 2011 for the 2011/2012 award year).

2. Be a graduate or professional student.

3. Be married or separated on the date he or she files the aid application (engagements and upcoming divorces do not affect status).

4. Have children who receive more than half of their support from you.

5. Have legal dependents (other than children or a spouse) who live with you and receive more than half of their support from you.

6. Be an orphan, ward of the court, or in foster care (at any time after turning 13 years of age.)

7. Be an emancipated minor, or in legal guardianship (as determined by a court); or an unaccompanied youth who is homeless, or at risk for homelessness.

8. Be a veteran of the U.S. Armed Forces; or be serving on active duty in the U.S. Armed Forces (for purposes other than training).

9. Be judged independent by the financial aid administrator based on documented unusual circumstances.

A Very, Very Important Point

OK, you say. I am eligible to apply. But why should I? I'll never qualify for federal aid. My family makes too much money. We own prime real estate near Guffey, Colorado. So why bother with the paperwork? There are three answers to this question.

One—A lot of government employees and contractors make their living processing forms. If applications came only from people who qualify for awards, their work load would be cut in half. There would be a drastic increase in lay-offs and unemployment. Do you want to be responsible for increasing our nation's unemployment figures?

Two—Colleges expect you to apply. They don't know this book exists. They assume the only way you can figure out if you qualify is to run through the application drill. As they see it, Uncle Sam offers an unlimited amount of federal aid, and they want to make absolutely certain you bring your share of that money to Frugal U. In fact, most colleges feel so strongly about this, they won't consider you for other aid unless you can prove you applied for federal aid and were turned down, or you have need beyond that covered by federal aid.

Three—Your state expects you to apply. It, too, feels strongly about this and may not consider you eligible for state programs unless you've applied for federal aid.

We know our first answer did not inspire you to apply. But our last two answers should—if you want to receive any aid at all.

A Tip For the Men

Have you registered for Selective Service? It is a prerequisite for qualifying for federal student aid and Congress has announced, in a loud, clear fashion, that federal aid will be denied to young men age 18 to 25 who are not registered.

You can register via the FAFSA (see below), or online at **www.sss.gov**. If you want to confirm your registration, or your exemption status, you can reach Selective Service at 847/688-6888.

Applying for Federal Student Aid

You apply for federal student aid using a **FAFSA** (Free Application for Federal Student Aid). A central processor matches your application information against several national databases to verify your eligibility for aid. For example, it checks your Selective Service status, your Social Security number, your citizenship status, and your financial aid history (to make sure you're not in default on any student loans). The processor also checks your data for inconsistencies and contradictions.

Next, the processor evaluates your finances, calculates your "Expected Family Contribution" (EFC) and incorporates your EFC into an eligibility document called a Student Aid Report (SAR). Finally, the processor sends you a copy of your SAR and transmits your data to all the schools you designate on your FAFSA, your state higher education agency and the state higher education agencies of all the schools you list on your FAFSA.

You may use the appendices to get a close estimate of your EFC.

Paper FAFSAs

In the fall, students may call the Federal Student Aid Information Center, (800/4-FED-AID) and request up to three paper copies of the FAFSA. (Forms will no longer be supplied to high school guidance offices.) *Uncle Sam also prints the application in Spanish.* You fill out the FAFSA as soon after January 1 as possible and snail mail it to the address listed on the form. You pay no fee.

The 2011/2012 FAFSA will be purple and yellow.

FAFSA on the Web (www.fafsa.gov)

Students may also use FAFSA on the Web (www.fafsa.gov) in either English or Spanish to file an electronic FAFSA directly with the central processor. Uncle continues to enhance his online application and reports that nearly all forms are now filed electronically.

FAFSA on the Web includes worksheets, online help, detailed instructions and an EFC Estimator, however, families won't see their estimated EFC until *AFTER* they submit their form. FAFSA on the Web also includes internal edits that help prevent errors and reduce rejections. Finally, parents with multiple students in college can transfer their parental data to additional FAFSA applications with the click of a mouse.

At the FAFSA web site, families can print a pre-application worksheet to collect data and make it easier (and faster) to complete your FAFSA online.

Paper FAFSAs take four weeks to process; electronic FAFSAs take only one. *If possible, save time and file electronically.* Don't view this as a chance to procrastinate. Consider it a two-week head start on your equally-needy, but technophobic classmates. Save often (in case you get bumped off-line), and in your eagerness, don't click "SEND" until you've checked your answers carefully!

Also, don't be confused by www.FAFSA.com. This enterprising financial aid consultant nabbed a prime domain name, but charges families to complete the forms. If you want to pay for their services, that's fine. But you can do it yourself for free. Your choice.

Recent Form Changes

There has been quite a bit of discussion over the increasing length and complexity of the FAFSA; it now has over 100 questions and Congress is concerned that it's intimidating the very people it is supposed to help—millions of low-income undergraduates are not applying for aid.

As part of the ongoing "simplification" effort, the Department of Education eliminated two questions from the paper FAFSA this year, but added one, to gather information about a student's high school. The simplification effort has been more successful with the online FAFSA—it uses "skip logic" so students can bypass questions that aren't relevant. Another good reason to complete the form online.

Personal Identification Numbers (www.pin.ed.gov)

If you want to file your FAFSA online, apply now for a "Personal Identification Number" (PIN) which will act as your electronic signature. (No need to wait until January 1.) Otherwise, you have to print and snail mail the FAFSA signature page, thus losing out on some benefits of electronic filing.

Not only does your PIN verify your identity when completing a FAFSA, you can use it later to track the status of your application, make online corrections, or even to review your entire financial aid history. You request PINs directly from the Department of Education (www.pin.ed.gov).

If your parents must sign the FAFSA, they need to have their own (separate) PIN.

Fafsa4Caster (www.fafsa4caster.ed.gov)

A good way to get a head start on the process is to use Fafsa4Caster. Prior to January 1, families can use this tool to receive an early estimate of their eligibility for federal student aid. Even better, when you start work on your FAFSA, much of the data you entered using Fafsa4Caster will be transferred to the real form.

Renewal FAFSAs

You must re-apply for aid every year. If you filed a FAFSA in 2010/2011, you will receive a Renewal Reminder Notice in early January that provides instructions about how to reapply for aid using Renewal FAFSA on the Web. (Renewal FAFSAs must all be filed online.) Some of the fields will be "pre-populated" with data you provided last year, so unless there's a change in information, you can skip some of the questions.

The renewal reminder notice will be sent to the e-mail address you listed on your 2010/2011 FAFSA. If you did not include a valid e-mail address, or the e-mail is undeliverable, you will receive a paper reminder.

Applying for Collegiate Aid

The focus of this publication is on federal student aid, but we don't want you to miss out on the other large source of financial aid—money from your college. Over 60% of all four-year private colleges, and over one-quarter of all four-year public colleges, require a second aid application to determine eligibility for collegiate aid. Unfortunately, there is no single, standard form or formula. Some schools have developed their own application to gather additional knowledge about your family's finances. Others use the College Board's Financial Aid PROFILE. Some schools use both.

Financial Aid PROFILE

The basic PROFILE requires the same sort of data as the FAFSA, with a few extra questions about income, assets, expenses, and resources. But the College Board has accumulated nearly 200 additional questions that schools may ask. These questions pry into everything from the student's career objective, to whether the student has applied for outside scholarships, to whether the family has recently sold any income generating assets (and the purpose for which they were sold), to the year, make and model of all the family's motor vehicles. PROFILE can also include a business/farm supplement and collect information on the noncustodial parent.

PROFILE information should be in your guidance office this September. If you're applying to one of the 250+ PROFILE schools, you must register and complete the form online (profileonline.collegeboard.com)—it will be customized with each of your school's questions.

You'll also find extensive online help at profileonline.collegeboard.com.

Unfortunately, you have to pay a fee for all this fun; $25 to register (which includes one school report) then $16 for each additional school or program that is to receive your information. Students from low income families may receive a fee waiver for up to six reports.

Schools cannot require you to file PROFILE to be considered for federal student aid, but they can require it before awarding aid from their own resources. Lesson: Find out which schools require what forms to make sure you're considered for every aid source possible.

Also, you may file PROFILE well before January 1, which helps colleges get a head start on estimating financial aid packages. Check the filing deadlines carefully—registration for PROFILE may begin as early as October 1 with schools receiving results in early November.

When to Submit the FAFSA

Right after January 1, but not before. You'll need to have your income tax information close at hand. Certain items on your aid application and the income tax form will have to agree right down to the last decimal. Most importantly: your family's Adjusted Gross Income, the amount of federal income taxes paid, family size, and number of dependents. Up to 30% of all applications are checked against income tax return. Some schools ask every student for copies of the family's 1040—just to keep people honest.

These odds create quite a dilemma. The IRS says you don't have to file tax forms until April 15. Many people wait until the last minute claiming to work most efficiently under pressure. We think it's because they want to be filmed by a TV crew when they join the line outside the post office at 11:59pm on April 15th. Important: If you wait that long to do your income tax and student aid application, it won't matter if the numbers match. Even though the final FAFSA deadline for the 2011/2012 year is not until June 30, 2012, you will have missed the deadlines set by most colleges.

Our advice: Don't wait until April 15th—if you really are pressed for time, file for aid using estimated information. You will then be asked, later on, to provide copies of your signed tax forms for verification. If the numbers match, the estimate will survive. Otherwise, there will be a recalculation. Lesson: Even an estimate must be accurate.

A Good Use of the Winter Holiday

To make sure you're one of the early birds, start collecting the necessary financial records over the winter holidays. Print a copy of the FAFSA on the Web worksheet to help you gather the correct information (but please don't submit the worksheet in lieu of a FAFSA—it's not an official document).

Assembling Information for the Application

Start collecting the information you need to fill out the application form (as well as to do your income taxes) as soon as possible. You'll need to know:

- Taxable income for both parents and students, including wages, pensions, capital gains, rents, interest, dividends, annuities, unemployment compensation, alimony received and business income.
- Non-taxable income, including worker's compensation, housing and food allowances, child support payments received, untaxed pensions and IRA distributions, veteran's non-education benefits, tax-exempt interest income, and earned income credit.
- The value of cash, savings, and checking accounts (as of the day you plan to sign the application) for both parents and the student.
- The net worth of other investments: stocks, bonds, commodities, precious metals, trusts, and college savings plan. Again, this information should be as of the date you sign the application.
- The market value of real estate other than your home. Creative financing has artificially inflated the market value of much real estate. You may not want to use recent transaction prices as true guides, but go for a somewhat more conservative valuation.

Accuracy

In completing the form, be as accurate as you can. If you don't understand something, call Uncle Sam at 800-4-FED-AID, or ask a guidance counselor or financial aid administrator. Many colleges now have toll free numbers for exactly that purpose.

Once you complete the form, sign it. If you are a dependent student, at least one of your parents must sign as well. File online if possible. Otherwise, mail the paper FAFSA to the address on the form and nowhere else.

What Happens Next?

In due time (three weeks if you filed a paper application; one week for an online application) the people who own the computer that processes your form will prepare a document, called a **Student Aid Report** or SAR.

- If you recorded an e-mail address on your FAFSA (whether you used a paper form, or FAFSA on the Web), you will receive an e-mail with a link to an online SAR which you can access by providing your social security number, date of birth, and first two letters of your last name.

- If you didn't record an e-mail address, and you used a paper FAFSA, you will receive a paper SAR in the mail.

- If you didn't record an e-mail address, and you used FAFSA on the Web, you will receive a SAR Information Acknowledgment—it provides less detailed information than the SAR, and cannot be used to make corrections.

The Student Aid Report (SAR)

The first part of the SAR displays your Expected Family Contribution (upper right hand corner) and information about your eligibility status, verification requirements (see below) and instructions on how to correct any mistakes or assumptions made during processing.

The second part of the SAR displays the information upon which your EFC is based. The order of the data elements follows the same order as the FAFSA. If, based on reading this book, you thought your EFC should be $500 and now you learn that it's $5,000, you may want to check the information summary carefully to see if you or the computer got a decimal point in the wrong place.

If anything is incorrect under the "You Told Us" column, cross it out and enter the correct data in the "Corrected Items Only" column. For example, if you reported taxable income rather than AGI, now is the time to make that correction.

Also, if anything is missing, you must provide the missing data so your eligibility can be recalculated. After making corrections or supplying missing information, the student (and parents for dependent students) signs the form and returns it for reprocessing.

If you have a PIN, you can use FAFSA Corrections on the Web (www.fafsa.gov), to make all of these corrections online.

Note: You may not use this form to provide new information, i.e., you may not change the value of your assets to reflect a different worth than as of the date you filed your original application.

SAR Information Acknowledgment

If you complete the FAFSA online you will receive an SAR Information Acknowledgment. Like the SAR described above, this acknowledgment contains information on your eligibility status as well as a summary of the information used to calculate your EFC. Review this information carefully, and if you need to make corrections, you can do so (using your PIN) at Fafsa on the Web (www.fafsa.gov).

Verification

If your EFC has an asterisk next to it, you are a candidate for verification which means the financial aid administrator might need to substantiate the data you provided in your application before awarding you any aid. For more on verification, see Chapter 3.

"Eligible" and "Ineligible" Students

At the same time the processor sends you your SAR, it transmits to your school an equivalent document called an Institutional Student Information Record (ISIR). If the student is *eligible* for a Pell Grant, the school may use this ISIR to report that fact to Uncle's Pell Grant Disbursement System. That's how the school gets its money. If the student is *ineligible* for a Pell Grant, the school may start building an aid package using other resources.

"Rejected" Students

In addition to eligible and ineligible students, there are also "rejected" students whose eligibility cannot be calculated because the application contained too much inconsistent information. Examples: A blank or invalid date of birth (many students accidently put the current year), a missing name, an incorrect social security number, or illegible data. Part 2 of that student's SAR is called an "Information Request Form." If you follow its instructions for providing missing data and submit it for reprocessing, you can become an "eligible" or "ineligible" student.

Regardless of how students apply, they will receive a rejected paper SAR if a student or parent signature is missing.

Applying to More than Four Schools

If you apply online, you may ask to have your data sent to ten colleges. Unfortunately, the paper FAFSA only has space for you to list four colleges; if you are applying to more than four, here are some suggested strategies:

1. List the four schools with the earliest deadlines. If you start the process early, you have plenty of time to get your data to the others.
2. List your top four schools. If you're running short on time, make sure your preferred colleges get your information first.
3. List the four most expensive colleges. If you will need financial aid (beyond the unlimited amounts provided by Uncle Sam) to afford the school, make sure the pricey schools get your data before they run out of institutional aid.
4. List public colleges first, then private institutions—a reverse of the advice above. Most private colleges use PROFILE and/or their own financial questionnaire to get the same information, and they can use this information to begin estimating your eligibility for financial aid.
5. List in-state schools first (public and private), to increase your chances of receiving money from your home state.

Whichever rationale you choose, you can add additional schools once you receive your Student Aid Report (SAR).

Meanwhile, Back at the Financial Aid Office

Once the aid administrator knows your eligibility status he or she can start building your aid package—the combination of awards that makes up the difference between what college costs and what you can pay. If you are eligible for a Pell, it becomes the bottom layer of the package. If you are not eligible, the FAA must look somewhere else.

Questions—Problems

Useful Phone Contacts

For information about federal programs, call the Federal Student Aid Information Center, 800/4-FED-AID, from 8am to midnight, EST, seven days a week (TTY: 800/730-8913). Trained staff can help you:

• Complete the FAFSA
• Check on the status of your FAFSA
• Make corrections to your Student Aid Report (SAR)
• Request a duplicate SAR
• Explain Expected Contribution
• Answer questions about eligibility

You may also request Uncle's free book, *Funding Education Beyond High School*. (Blind and visually-impaired students may request audio highlights of the book on a compact disc.) The number is NOT to be used for financial counseling, to interpret policy, or to expedite application processing.

Questions about electronic applications: For technical help with electronic FAFSAs and electronic Renewal FAFSAs, call 800/801-0576.

Useful Web Contacts

The Federal Student Aid Home Page (studentaid.ed.gov) is a good starting place for gathering information. You can view the site in English or Spanish. It includes links to FAFSA on the Web and Federal School Codes. (You record your schools' codes on your FAFSA so Uncle knows where to send your need analysis results.) It also includes links to:

- *Completing the FAFSA* (studentaid.ed.gov) which provides very detailed FAFSA instructions, in English or Spanish.

- *Funding Education Beyond High School: The Guide to Federal Student Aid* (studentaid.ed.gov) which answers all your basic questions about federal student aid, in English or Spanish. Blind and visually-impaired students can hear highlights at www.FederalStudentAid.ed.gov/audio.

Information for Financial Aid Professionals (IFAP) *Library* (www.ifap.ed.gov) is for people who work in the student aid field, or families with an interest in the nitty-gritty of student aid regulations, including all of Uncle's "Dear Colleague" letters and "Negotiated Rulemaking" sessions.

Students.Gov (www.students.gov) was designed to be a 24/7 "Student Gateway to the U.S. Government." Its collection of (commercial and governmental) sites helps students find a job (or internship), e-file taxes, plan vacations, register to vote, buy postage stamps, and plan and pay for a college education.

College.gov (www.college.gov) is a new site, still being developed by the Department of Education. It is intended to be the federal government's main source for information about planning, preparing and paying for college.

Using the USPS

If you decide to apply using paper forms and snail mail, protect yourself against postal loss. (1) Make copies of anything you plan to entrust to the mail. (2) Apply online whenever possible. Not only will your information get to its destination much faster, your data has less chance of being interpreted incorrectly by a mere mortal.

CHAPTER 2

■■■■■■■■■■■■■■■■■■■

SPECIAL SITUATIONS AND
SPECIAL CONDITIONS

Special Situations

Once upon a time, Dad went off to work every morning and Mom stayed home to cook, clean, and take care of the kids. This kind of family is rapidly disappearing. Less than 15% of all households are what used to be called "normal." Here is how you handle "special" situations on financial aid application forms.

Divorce or Separation

If the applicant's parents divorce or separate before the student applies for aid, the student must report the income of the parent with whom he or she lived for the greater portion of the 12 months preceding the date of application.

If the student did not live with either parent, or spent an equal amount of time with each parent, the student must report the income information of the parent who provided the greater amount of financial support during the 12 months preceding the date of application.

"Financial support" includes cash, food, clothing, housing, medical or dental care, and contribution to college costs.

Remarriage

If the applicant's parent remarries before the application is filed, the student must report the stepparent's income and asset information. There are no exceptions to this rule. Prenuptial agreements or disclaimers of support from the stepparent are not acceptable.

Death

If a parent dies before the student applies for federal aid, the student should report only the income and assets of the living parent, even though the tax return shows both parents' incomes.

If both parents die, or the remaining parent dies before the student applies, the student is considered independent and uses the Independent Student worksheets to determine aid eligibility.

Job Loss

If you have recently lost your job, or received a lay-off notice, you might qualify as a "dislocated worker" and be eligible for the Simplified Needs Test (which excludes assets) or an Auto-Zero EFC. The FAFSA now captures these situations if they occur before you file (Question 83 on the paper FAFSA).

Parents Who Refuse to Provide Information

If you truly don't have access to parental resources, complete the FAFSA as best you can (e.g., without including parental data). You will be allowed to submit the form, but you will only be considered eligible for unsubsidized federal student loans. Solution? Let your colleges know about your situation, and what you've done on the FAFSA. Many students today come from non-traditional families and schools are becoming experts at wading through prickly situations to be as fair as possible. The school might decide to override your status and allow you to apply for aid as an "Independent Student."

Why is the system so strict about this? If students whose parents refused to provide information got lots of student aid, everyone's parents might start refusing to provide information.

There are, however, three situations in which your high school counselor or college financial aid administrator can sign in place of your parents.

1. Your parents reside outside the United States and can't be contacted by "normal" means.
2. You don't know where your parents are (and we don't mean they've been gone for a half-hour, and you want to send your form off at that particular moment).
3. Your parents are determined (by proper authority) to be physically or mentally incapable of signing the application.

Special Conditions

The above paragraphs cover special situations that exist before you submit the FAFSA. For events that occur after you submit the application (special conditions), you'll have to speak with the aid administrator.

"Professional Judgment"

Schools may use "professional judgment" to make three kinds of adjustments in determining your eligibility for federal student aid:

- *First*, they may change your student status from dependent to independent, provided you give them convincing reason.
- *Second*, they may re-calculate your Expected Family Contribution. Schools aren't allowed to change the Federal Methodology formula, or adjust your "bottom line" EFC directly, but they can modify the data

elements used in the calculation, for example, lower the value of your assets, or use expected year income, rather than prior year. Of course, they may wait until Spring semester to adjust your award, so they can examine your 2011 tax return.

- *Third*, they may adjust the components of your cost of attendance figure. For example, if you have an unusually expensive commute, they may increase your transportation allowance.

A survey done by The College Board and the National Association of Student Financial Aid Administrators showed that "professional judgment" was generally based on a combination of written need analysis policies and the staff member's own judgment. Eleven percent of all reviewed cases resulted in a change in dependency status; thirty-seven percent resulted in a lower Expected Family Contribution, and ten percent resulted in a higher cost of attendance.

If you feel your family contribution is too high, or your cost of attendance too low, and you are able to prove your case (for example, you face one of the situations described below) please contact the financial aid administrator. If you aren't truly "needy," we hope you'll be content with using low interest loan money to pay the bills, thus preserving scarce grant money for families who are less well-off.

Be aware, some reviews lead to higher expected family contributions and lower costs of attendance. Lesson. Make sure your facts back up your case.

Special Conditions for Dependent Students

What counts as a special condition? There is no defined list of situations that qualify, but the following items should give you the idea. In general, "special condition" is synonymous with "unpleasant condition," or events relating to death, divorce, unemployment and natural disasters.

1. A parent or stepparent whose 2010 income from work must be reported became unemployed in 2011.

2. A parent or stepparent who received some form of nontaxable income or benefit in 2010 lost that income or benefit in 2011. Nontaxable income and benefits include: untaxed social security benefits, court-ordered child support payments, nontaxable retirement or disability payments, welfare benefits, and Aid to Families with Dependent Children.

3. A parent or stepparent whose 2010 income from work must be reported has been unable to pursue normal income-producing activities during 2011 because of a disability or a natural disaster (usual examples: floods, hurricanes, and earthquakes).

4. A parent or stepparent whose 2010 income must be reported dies after the student files a regular application.

5. Parents divorce or separate after the student files a regular application.

6. The student's last surviving parent dies after the student files an application. In that case, the student becomes an independent student.
7. The family has unreimbursed medical expenses that exceed 3½% of their adjusted gross income.
8. The student has younger siblings enrolled in private secondary schools.

Special Conditions for Independent Students

1. An applicant who worked full-time in 2010 is no longer employed full-time in 2011. This is intended to help the applicant who leaves work to return to school.
2. An applicant's spouse whose 2010 income from work must be reported became unemployed for at least ten weeks in 2011.
3. An applicant or applicant's spouse who received some form of nontaxable income or benefit in 2010 lost that income or benefit in 2011. Nontaxable income and benefits include: untaxed social security benefits, court-ordered child support payments, nontaxable retirement or disability payments, welfare benefits, and Aid to Families with Dependent Children.
4. An applicant or applicant's spouse whose 2010 income from work must be reported has been unable to pursue normal income-producing activities during 2011 because of a disability or a natural disaster (for example: floods, hurricanes and earthquakes).
5. An applicant divorces or separates after filing the original application.
6. The applicant's spouse whose 2010 income must be reported dies after the applicant files a regular application.
7. The applicant or applicant's spouse has unreimbursed medical expenses that exceed 3½% of the combined adjusted gross income.
8. The applicant has dependents enrolled in private secondary schools.

Other Considerations

Don't try to explain away high vacation expenses, or a sibling's five-star wedding, or the necessity of a newly remodeled kitchen. But do note legitimate "involuntary" expenses or unusual situations that might convince an aid administrator to re-evaluate your contribution. Here are some additional questions to ask yourself:

- Has your College Fund declined significantly in value since the date you filed your aid application?
- Is one of your parents about to retire? Do they have a skimpy retirement fund?
- Are your parents repaying their own student loans, or those of an older sibling?
- Are your parents helping an older sibling with graduate school?

- Do you have consumer debt resulting from past unemployment?
- Do you have high child care costs?
- Have you received notice that you will soon be laid off?
- Is your contribution from student income figure inflated because you took a year off to work?
- Is your contribution from student assets inflated because the family saved its money in the student's name? Did the parent put it there? Or did it come from some other source, like grandparents, aunts or uncles?
- Is your contribution from parental income figure inflated because of a one-time, unexpected bonus or capital gain? Is that money being double-counted as an asset, as well?
- Will you be attending camp (for example, in dance or tennis) or serving the community in lieu of taking a paying summer job?
- Did you pay more in state and local taxes than need analysis allowed?
- Are your parents paying nursing home costs for their own parents?
- Did the school exclude consideration of your Hope or Lifetime Learning tax credits?
- Do you have siblings attending expensive private colleges (who received less-than-generous aid packages)?
- Are your retirement assets all "out in the open," rather than hidden in a 401(k), IRA or Keogh?
- Do you live in a region with a high cost of living, like New York City or San Francisco?
- Is your new business eating up assets, rather than generating income?
- Are you an independent student who was required to report parental income and assets on the aid application?

CHAPTER 3

....

VERIFICATION, OUCH!

Dear Student:

"Your aid application indicated you were married, but listed a household size of one. Your most recent income tax return listed you as single with two dependent children. Please explain all this and give us the correct information."

This fictional student is a candidate for verification. But your application does not have to be nearly this confused to require verification.

How Are Forms Selected for Verification?

When the processor receives your FAFSA, in addition to calculating EFC, it checks for inconsistencies and flags those with "questionable information," for example, a family that reports a very low income figure relative to the amount of taxes paid, a family that reports a very low income figure yet has no earned income credit, or a dependent student who reports his parents' marital status as "married" but household size as "two."

The processor also matches FAFSA information to other databases to catch students who have defaulted on loans, whose names don't correspond with their social security number, whose citizenship status is in question, or who should have, but didn't register for the draft.

Finally, the processor will let the aid administrators know which forms have been "edit-selected for verification" which is bureaucratese for "these forms smell rotten." A look at your EFC should tell you if you are one of the lucky ones to be verified. If it has an asterisk, you know you've won something. If it has a "C," you know it's the grand prize! The computer has identified an eligibility problem that must be resolved before any student aid may be awarded. The aid office will want to see all sorts of documentation (including a copy of your income tax return).

What Items Must the FAA Verify?

Verification is performed by the overworked aid administrator at the school you will attend. At a minimum, verification will include household size, number enrolled in college, adjusted gross income, US income taxes paid, and certain untaxed income and benefits (for example, social security benefits, child support received, payments to IRA/Keogh plans, interest on tax-free bonds, and earned income credit). But it can cover other areas, as well. It may require verification of a student's claim to being "independent." If the aid administrator doesn't want to stop here, verification can go further, to cover every item on the application, welfare benefits, housing allowances, business value, trust funds, investment property. You'll have to provide a copy of your final US Income Tax return as well as whatever additional documentation is requested.

If, after the checking, your household is as you claimed, and your numbers are within certain tolerance limits, there is no need to reprocess the form. If you are outside the limits, the FAA must recalculate your family contribution.

Tolerance Levels

If the total differences between your AGI, untaxed income and US income taxes paid as reported on your original FAFSA and as submitted for verification are $400 or less, the financial aid administrator need not recalculate your EFC. For example, if your actual AGI is $500 higher than you originally reported, and your taxes paid are $100 more than you originally reported, your net tolerance is $400 and the financial aid administrator need not take further action.

		On FAFSA	Verification
	AGI	$30,000	$30,500
+	Untaxed Income	0	0
−	Taxes Paid	$3,000	$3,100
		$27,000	$27,400

There is no tolerance at all for differences in non-dollar items like household size. If there's a discrepancy, the financial aid administrator must recalculate the family's expected contribution.

Completing Verification

Verification is a hassle for the applicant and for the aid administrator, but with up to 30% of all applications selected each year, odds are you will go through the process. So we say again: Be honest and accurate in filling out the forms. Make sure the FAFSA items that correspond to income tax items are identical. And, make sure you have back-up documentation for other statements you make, such as the status of your assets. Then, if the aid office requests the information, you can run it through a copy machine and send it off.

CHAPTER 4

■■■■■■■■■■■■■■■■■■■■

MEET YOUR FRIENDLY PELL GRANT

What Is a Pell?

The Pell Grant used to be called the Basic Educational Opportunity Grant or BEOG. But in an eponymous mood (look this word up for an extra ten points on your SAT), Congress decided to rename the program in honor of the distinguished (retired) senator from Rhode Island, Claiborne Pell, who introduced, and won legislative approval for this form of assistance.

Pells, as they are now known, are a huge and broad-based program. About $35.8 billion will be dispensed to over 9.4 million students in 2011/2012 with an average award equal to $3,800. Most recipients come from families with incomes under $50,000. You should be aware, however, that the program is complex in design. It is subject to frequent rule changes. And, when all is said and done, your grant may be less than you had expected.

But don't be put off by such cynicism, the Pell Grant program does work. Money does materialize. And it can flow right into your pocket.

Who Are Pells For?

Pells are for undergraduates only. They represent the foundation of all financial aid packages presented to students whose ability to pay college bills falls short of college costs. You may receive a Pell for up to 18 semesters of undergraduate education. And, students who are accelerating completion of their degrees by enrolling year-round may receive up to two Pell awards in an academic year. On top of the Pell, students often receive additional aid—state grants, scholarships, work programs, and loans.

How Much Are Pells Worth?

For 2011/2012, the President budgeted for a maximum Pell of $5,550. The minimum Pell equals 10% of the maximum Pell funded for that year. Students who are eligible for a Pell that is between 5% and 10% of the maximum Pell shall receive the minimum (10%) Pell. Students eligible for less than 5% receive nothing.

How large a Pell will you get? It varies with your Expected Family Contribution (EFC) and your school's cost of attendance. Pells, when combined with your EFC, cannot exceed the cost of college.

- If your school costs more than the maximum Pell, your grant will approximate the maximum Pell minus your EFC. *Example*: If the cost of college is $15,000, and the maximum Pell is $5,550, an EFC of $1,000 translates into a $4,550 Pell.
  (Calculation: $5,550 – $1,000 = $4,545)

- If your school costs less than the maximum Pell, your grant will approximate that cost minus your EFC. *Example*: If the cost of college is $3,000, an EFC of $1,300 translates into a $1,700 Pell.
  (Calculation: $3,000 – $1,300 = $1,700)

We say "approximate" because aid administrators use payment schedules that show the exact amounts, rounded to the nearest $50 or $100.

Also, if the top award is $5,550, you should know that students who qualify for between $275 and $555 receive $555. Students who qualify for between $0 and $275 get nothing. Eligible students will be those with EFCs ranging from $0 to about $5,275. (Throughout this chapter, we have assumed a top award of $5,550, but with the FY2012 budget not yet settled, keep your eyes and ears open!)

Beginning with the 2011/2012 academic year, the maximum authorized Pell is supposed to be indexed to the CPI plus 1 percent, with an estimated maximum grant of $6,900 by 2019. But remember, there is a big difference between "authorized limits" and "funded limits"—each $100 increase in the maximum Pell costs the government at least $560 million, and probably more. A weak labor market usually leads to increasing numbers of Pell eligible students going to school, and a corresponding explosion of Pell costs.

Variables You Must Consider

In actuality, several variables influence the size of the award. These variables include award reductions if you are less than a full-time student, congressional actions that remove dollars from amounts already appropriated, and appropriations that are not large enough to fund all entitlements.

Add these variables up, and you will become a cynic at an age when you should still believe that good triumphs over evil and getting up early in the morning makes you healthy, wealthy, and wise.

Variable #1—When You Are Less Than a Full-Time Student

If you qualify for an award, the size of the award will correspond to the percentage of the load you take. If you are a part-time, half-time or three-quarter time student, you receive 25%, 50% or 75% of your award, respectively. Let's illustrate:

- **Bob L. Head** is a half-time student studying sports marketing. Her Family Contribution is $1,000. Assuming the maximum Pell Grant is $5,550, Bob qualifies for an award of 50% of $4,550 or $2,275.

- **Matilda Waltz** is a three-quarter-time student studying dance at Ozzie State. Her Family Contribution is $0 which qualifies her for the maximum grant. Matilda's award? 75% of $5,550 or $4,162.50
- **Bruce Driver** is a part-time student at United Pacific State. His Family Contribution is $4,950. Bruce's award? It is 25% of $600 or $150. Since this is less than the minimum grant, Bruce gets nothing. If his Family Contribution had been $0, he would have gotten 25% of $5,550 or $1,387.50. (Note: all part-time students receive about 25% of a full award, no matter how many courses they take.)

Variable #2—Taking Money Out of the Program

Year in and year out, politicians demonstrate their concern for the public by talk of "balancing the budget" or "cutting spending." To accomplish this, they can remove (or "rescind") money already appropriated. One year, for instance, they sliced $140 million off the Pell appropriation. Congress then had to reduce all awards already authorized by shaving each one by $50.

The good news is Congress doesn't always go after the Pell program. One year, they took billions out of the education budget, but salved their consciences by increasing the maximum Pell by $30.

Variable #3—Insufficient Appropriations

Legislators take a healthy guess at how many people will apply for aid, how many of those who apply will be eligible for Pells under whatever rules are in effect that day, and what the average-size grant will be. Based on that guess, legislators appropriate money for the program. If more students than expected apply and prove eligible, and the individual awards are to be larger than anticipated, the money in the program will not stretch. In some years, the shortfall has exceeded $1 billion.

When the Pell program has shortfalls Congress can (1) vote to appropriate more money; (2) trim the top award by a few hundred dollars, or (3) fiddle with the EFC formula so fewer (middle-income) students are eligible.

Where Can the Awards Be Used?

Pells can be used at any of the 7,000+ colleges, universities, vo-tech schools, or schools of nursing that take part in federal financial aid programs. All these schools must be accredited by an approved accrediting agency. Before enrolling at any school, a student should determine whether or not it is an accredited participant in Uncle Sam's aid programs.

Distance Education Courses

You may also be able to qualify for a Pell Grant if you are enrolled in a distance education course provided the program is accredited. For help in determining the legitimacy of an online degree program, check out the Council for Higher Education Accreditation, www.chea.org.

The subject of online courses continues to be studied more thoroughly by Congress—the government must figure out how to get money to legitimate students, yet prevent fraud. Uncle worries about virtual schools enrolling virtual students with real Pells. To be safe, limit your online study to e-courses from established institutions with bricks and mortar campuses.

Jail

You can even qualify for a Pell if you are incarcerated in a local jail (but not a state or federal correctional institution). Your cost of attendance figure is limited to tuition, fees and books—it does not include room or board because they are generously provided by the inmate's host institution.

> **Linda Lockenstock** is in a local jail for the unauthorized photocopying of this publication. She decides to study copyright law (full-time). Lockenstock qualifies for a maximum Pell of $5,550. Tuition at Ironfence U. is only $2,000. Since Pells, combined with your EFC can't exceed your cost of attendance, Lockenstock receives a $2,000 grant.

CHAPTER 5
■■■■■■■■■■■■■■■■■■■

LOANS, LOANS, LOANS, LOANS. . .

The Role of Uncle Sam

Here is the good news about Uncle Sam. He helps students get college loans below the current interest rate. In some cases, he will even pay the interest while the student is in school. He will guarantee loans against default. He will cancel loans if the borrower dies, becomes totally disabled, or goes into bankruptcy. And, he will permit loan deferment while the borrower does worthwhile things like giving smallpox vaccines to headhunters in New Guinea.

Now here is the bad news. Uncle will tamper with his programs. He will change interest rates when least expected. He will widen eligibilities one year and restrict access the next. He will invent new forms. He will write incomprehensible regulations and design procedures that are impossible to follow. Finally, he will hire more staff to administer what he has wrought, and pay for expensive studies to tell him what he did. In other words, Uncle Sam runs his financial aid programs as he does the rest of the country, with a lot of paper and even more red tape. He won't change, no matter how many Paperwork Reduction Acts are passed, so you must learn to appreciate the good, and get used to the frustration.

An Overview of Federal Student Loans

No two federal programs have the same features. Interest rates differ. Total amounts you can borrow vary. The type of borrower (e.g., graduate student, undergraduate student) may be specified. In addition, some programs are based on need, others are open to everyone. Some programs are heavily subsidized, others are not. And finally, some programs come with a grace period, while others require you to begin repayment immediately.

Program Acronyms

You may need an interpretation of some of the acronyms and abbreviations Uncle uses for his student loans:

- *FFEL*—Federal Family Education Loan, which consists of subsidized and unsubsidized Staffords and PLUS Loans. These loans were made by commercial lenders. Beginning July 1, 2010 no new loans could be originated in this program.

- *FDSL*—Federal Direct Student Loan, which consists of Direct subsidized and unsubsidized Staffords and Direct PLUS Loans. These loans are made by the federal government.
- *Stafford Loans*—formerly GSL or Guaranteed Student Loan
- *PLUS*—PLUS Loans, it's a long story. See Chapter 7.
- *Perkins Loans*—formerly NDSL or National Direct Student Loans
- *HPSL*—Health Professions Student Loan

How Much Loan Money Is Available?

Stafford and PLUS are entitlement programs—there is no funding limit. The amount borrowed depends entirely on how many eligible students and parents seek out loans. Currently, Uncle has well over $300 billion in outstanding in student loans. You may read newspaper headlines like "Student Loan Program to be Cut by $X Billion." This number does not refer to the amount available to be borrowed, but rather the amount that Uncle pays to subsidize interest rates or gives to schools to cover administrative costs. Cutting these allowances reduces incentives and makes it more difficult for private lenders and schools to cover their expenses. Although some might abandon the program, if more money is needed to provide loans to eligible students, then, Congress must appropriate more money—or change the laws.

The amount in "revolving loan funds" (such as the Perkins program) depends on how much is appropriated each year and how responsible students are about repaying their outstanding loans.

Staffords and PLUS loans account for almost $95 billion in annual loans. Perkins Loans run around $1 billion dollars (and could increase to $5 - $6 billion next year). And medical loans contribute about $400 million.

Keeping Records

Students should set up a file to keep track of their student aid transactions, including all documents concerning their education loans. Most importantly, students should keep:

- Copies of correspondence with the lender, school and guarantor.
- A copy of their loan application, Promissory Note and Loan Disclosure Statement.
- A record of any loan checks received.
- A copy of their repayment schedule.
- A copy of request for forbearance (if necessary) or deferment.
- A record of all payments made by the borrower.
- The name of a contact person at the lender's.
- Entrance and exit interview forms

Mental Preparation for Indebtedness

In Romans (Chapter XII, Verse 8) we are told, "Owe no man anything." That is good advice. But in biblical times, there were no $40,000 schools. The Methusela Institute of Geriatrics never charged more than half a silver shekel per lunar semester. That low rate kept students out of the hands of the money-changers.

But today it's nearly impossible to get an education without going into debt. In fact, the average undergraduate debt now exceeds $18,000. In a way, this debt becomes a rite of passage to adulthood. When you think about it, in a predominantly middle class society, indebtedness is not only a normal condition, it is a necessity—like air and water. Our economy depends on it. Without debt, businesses would have no money for capital, and families would be without shelter, transportation—or vacations.

Students, however, may still not be aware of the sustaining power of borrowing. Their view of the future excludes the use of somebody else's money. To hear a typical child tell it:

"I have gone to school every day for sixteen years. I have had to listen to teachers every day for sixteen years. I have had homework every day for sixteen years. I can't wait to graduate and land a good job. Then I'll get my own apartment and a sports car. In the winter, I will ski at Crested Butte. In the summer I will scuba dive in the Bahamas. I am counting the days."

We say to this child, "You are right about counting. But count money, not days." Here is why. Say the child hit the jackpot and found a $35,000 per year job following graduation. Take home pay: about $2,100 per month. Let's look at that child's dream budget:

Apartment rental, utilities (including cable and cell phone)	$ 950.00
Monthly payment, used car	$ 150.00
Insurance, maintenance, gas	$ 150.00
Food, Sundries	$ 350.00
Clothing	$ 150.00
Miscellaneous	$ 100.00
Vacation fund	$ 50.00
Music and Entertainment	$ 150.00
MONTHLY PAYMENT ON $20,000 STUDENT LOAN	$ 218.00
TOTAL	**$2,268.00**

Something will have to give. And it won't be the student loan. Make your own dream budget. And then begin to scale it down. That's what we mean by mental preparation.

Experts recommend that student loan repayments not exceed 8 percent of your adjusted gross annual salary—on a $35,000 income that would be $2,800 or $233/month. Unfortunately, 25% of borrowers have loans in excess of 15% of their annual income.

Fear of Loans

Some people may require little more than mental preparation to enter the spirit of indebtedness. "Monthly payments" may have been their first words—after all, their baby furniture was purchased on credit. Mortgage burning parties were a neighborhood ritual. And the winters in Aruba meant summers with the bank loan officer.

Studies confirm that many people are afraid of loans. They did not grow up with them. Instead, going into debt was something to be avoided at all costs. Debt meant the surrender of freedom, and the possibility of more serious consequences. The study found an unwillingness to take out Stafford Loans, even though the students were eligible. Common questions included, "What happens if I can't find a job after graduation?" "How can I pay back then?" And, "What will they do to me if I can't pay it back?"

The answer: Quit worrying. Federal student loans have features that make them less frightening. For example:

1. You don't make any payments on a student loan until at least six months after you have completed your studies. That gives you half a year to find a job and earn good money.

2. If for some reason things don't work out and you haven't found a job, you are still protected. You can ask the lender for "forbearance." Forbearance means permission to stop making payments temporarily because you have problems—unemployment, poor health—that interfere with earning money.

3. Inflation works in your favor. The dollar you borrow is worth a lot more than the dollar you pay back.

Never, Never Default

Loans must be repaid. You must never default on a student loan. Defaulting is morally wrong as well as legally wrong.

It is morally wrong because not repaying a loan from a revolving fund can deprive a future college student from access to low-cost aid. That future student might be your brother or sister, or it might be your son or daughter. It is morally wrong because defaulting provides ammunition to those who feel federal student aid should be reduced or cut. And, it is morally wrong because you have in effect stolen money that did not belong to you.

Of course, defaulting is also legally wrong and the defaulter can end up in court. Currently, student loan defaults cost us over $2 billion each year as we (the taxpayers) must compensate for people who unilaterally decide to convert their loan to a grant. Back in 1990, default rates averaged 22.4%, but thanks to Uncle's increasing vigilance (and, maybe, a few bookkeeping changes), they now average only 7.2% overall—11.9% at trade schools; 6.2% at public colleges; and 4.1% at private colleges.

And who are these defaulters? A University of Kentucky researcher describes them as having two personality traits—low anxiety levels and a high tolerance for complexity in their lives. Translation: People who aren't likely to care about collection efforts. But here is what they can expect:

- Defaulters may see up to 10% of their wages garnished, until their loans are repaid. That percentage may soon increase to 15%.
- Defaulters may meet collection agencies and attorneys. Their property may be seized. They may end up in court. Their names may be given to the Justice Department (which prosecutes nearly 1,000 cases/year).
- Defaulters will receive a letter from the IRS explaining they will not receive a tax refund unless they negotiate a plan to pay off what they owe. Note: if you are filing a joint return, and your spouse is the defaulter, neither of you will receive a refund. Some states have instituted this policy when it comes to state refunds.
- Defaulters will be reported to credit bureaus. They may encounter difficulties in obtaining housing, automobile or business loans. The default will remain on your record for seven years.
- Colleges may refuse to provide defaulters with transcripts. As many employers require proof of academic achievement, this could impact on employment.

At this time, Uncle Sam is not quite in the same league as the Canadian Mounties. He doesn't always get his man—or woman. But, he is learning fast. And, with the help of IRS computers, he soon will. If you are in default, and want to set up a repayment schedule, call the Department of Education's Debt Collection Customer Service hotline at 800/621-3115.

Getting Out of Default

If you should find yourself in default, contact your lender to arrange some sort of repayment plan. You may be able to regain your borrowing privileges if you make on-time payments for six months.

CHAPTER 6

■■■■■■■■■■■■■■■■■■■

FEDERAL STAFFORD LOANS

Historical Perspective

Once upon a time, students had a hard time borrowing money. Bankers lend only against collateral—a house, savings, or tangible personal property. Students had no collateral and so they were unable to get loans.

Then Uncle Sam entered the picture. "Make the loans," he told the bankers, "and I will guarantee them. The United States is every student's collateral." It was a splendid idea. Uncle established a 7% interest rate on student loans—a figure that ran close to the prevailing interest rates. He also said he would pay the interest while the student was still in school. The program would cost the Treasury some money, but not too much.

This is not, however, a happily-ever-after story. Suddenly, interest rates took off to 12%, 15%, 18%, and 20% or more. This increased Uncle's costs from a few hundred million dollars per year to several billion for he had committed himself to (1) pay the interest on the loans while the student was enrolled and (2) pay the difference between 7% and the going interest rate during the repayment period. Critics of the program also pointed to all the savvy families who borrowed money at 7% while busily investing what should have been tuition money in Money Market accounts earning 17%. Uncle Sam tried to rein in what had fiscally become a runaway program.

In 1980, the interest rate was raised from 7% to 9%. In 1981, families were divided into two groups—those with incomes of $30,000 and under, and those with incomes of over $30,000. Eligibility requirements were established for each group and a loan origination fee was added.

Since that time, Uncle has eliminated the $30,000 threshold, and played with the interest rates and the fees—increasing them one year, decreasing them the next. In 1992, the rate was tied to the 91-day T-bill, and in 1993, the program was divided into two—subsidized loans for students with financial need, and unsubsidized loans for students without need. Students without need no longer receive interest subsidies while in school, or during the grace period before repayment.

Finally, in 2006, the interest rate was again changed, this time back to a fixed 6.8%, with a plan to reduce the rate to 3.4% over the next few years.

As you can see, the stability of the Stafford program corresponds directly to interest rates and the federal debt and deficit. If interest rates stay low and the national debt shrink, everyone will hail the program as Uncle's gift to students. If interest rates rise and the debt keeps growing, everyone will take steps to pass on part of the borrowing costs to students.

Parallel Universe

Another "innovation" was to create two parallel loan programs:

Federal Family Education Loans (FFEL) which consists of Subsidized Staffords, Unsubsidized Staffords and PLUS. These loans are made by commercial lenders; and

Federal Direct Student Loans (FDSL) which consists of Direct Subsidized Staffords, Direct Unsubsidized Staffords, and Direct PLUS. These loans are made by Uncle Sam.

Interest rates, loan limits, fees, deferments, cancellations, and forbearance terms are essentially the same. Repayment options vary slightly. The main difference, as far as the student is concerned, is who lends them the money.

So why are there two programs? For many years, there was a disagreement between elected officials over who best could run the programs—private lenders or Uncle Sam (with help from private contractors).

With a new Administration, and the recent troubles in the banking industry, Direct Lending gained the upper hand. Beginning July 1, 2010, all new federal student loans (Stafford and PLUS) must now be originated in the Direct Loan Program.

Stafford Loans: An Entitlement Program

The Stafford Loan is an entitlement program—there is no dollar ceiling set by Congress. Anybody and everybody who is eligible for a loan can get one. Currently, loan volume is running over $61 billion per year with over 14.5 million loans issued. By any informed guess, at least two million non-borrowers are eligible for subsidized loans (And, all non-borrowers qualify for at least a non-need based loan). So why don't they apply? Some may be following the wisdom of Shakespeare's Polonius, "Neither a borrower nor a lender be." But many more are just thoroughly confused by the constant changes in rules, eligibility requirements, and administrative details which have followed this program since its inception.

Program Summary

Federal Stafford Loans are low-interest loans to undergraduate and graduate students who are US citizens or resident aliens.

Students with financial need may receive a subsidized loan in which Uncle pays the interest while they are in school and during any deferments. *Students without financial need* may receive an unsubsidized loan in which interest accrues while they are in school and during any deferments. And finally, students may receive a combination of the two, the size of which depends on their student status and family income.

Loan Limits:

Dependent Undergraduates: Freshmen may borrow up to $3,500 per year. Sophomores may borrow $4,500 per year. Juniors, seniors and fifth-year undergrads may borrow $5,500 per year. If a student is borrowing under both the subsidized and unsubsidized program, these annual limits each increase by $2,000. For example, a freshman who receives a $1,500 subsidized Stafford may borrow an additional $4,000 under the unsubsidized program for a total of $5,500. The maximum undergraduate loan amount is $31,000 (of which no more than $23,000 can be subsidized).

Independent Undergraduates: Freshmen may borrow up to $3,500 per year. Sophomores may borrow $4,500 per year. Juniors, seniors and fifth-year undergrads may borrow $5,500 per year. If a student is borrowing under both the subsidized and unsubsidized program, these annual limits each increase by $6,000 for freshmen and sophomores and $7,000 for juniors, seniors and fifth-year undergraduates. The maximum an independent student may borrow during his or her undergraduate years is $57,500 (of which no more than $23,000 can be subsidized). Note: Dependent students whose parents have been turned down for a PLUS loan qualify for these higher limits as well.

Graduate Students may borrow up to $8,500 per year. If a student is borrowing under both the subsidized and unsubsidized program, this limit increases by $12,000 per year to a maximum of $138,500 (of which no more than $65,500 can be subsidized). This limit includes any money borrowed as an undergraduate. The Administration has proposed eliminating the interest subsidy on all graduate student loans beginning July 1, 2012.

Health Profession Students. Health Education Assistance Loans were discontinued. As a result, students in health-related fields may borrow increased amounts of unsubsidized Stafford money (up to $224,000).

Additional Limits. In no case may a Stafford Loan exceed the cost of attendance at your school minus any other financial aid you receive.

Prorated Loan Limits. Borrowing limits are prorated for programs of less than a full academic year, e.g., students attending the equivalent of one-third of an academic year are eligible for one-third of the maximum annual loan amount.

Interest Rate: The interest rate on subsidized loans is now fixed at 4.5% and will decrease to 3.4% for loans disbursed after July 1, 2011. Rates are set to increase to 6.8% beginning July 1, 2012. The interest rate on unsubsidized loans is already 6.8%.

Interest Subsidy. In the subsidized program, Uncle pays the interest while the student is enrolled and during the six-month grace period following completion of studies. In the unsubsidized program, students may forgo making payments, but interest continues to accrue. This interest is capitalized (added to the principal) only once—at the beginning of repayment.

Tip: If you have an unsubsidized loan, don't let the interest capitalize; instead, pay the interest while you're in school. The charges are minimal, and you'll save hundreds of dollars during repayment. Also, if your income is below the caps described in Chapter 10, you can deduct the interest payments from your AGI saving you tax dollars as well.

Grace Period. One grace period is permitted under the Stafford program—six months in length following completion of studies. There are no grace periods after subsequent deferments.

Who Makes Loans? Your loan goes straight from Uncle Sam to your university.

Eligible Schools: Accredited colleges and universities, vo-tech and trade schools; and eligible foreign schools. Over 7,000 total.

Question. What do I do if I've taken out an unsubsidized Stafford and I still need more money to pay for college? Are there other federal loan options?

Answer: Have your parents take out a PLUS loan (Chapter 7).

Income Requirements

Families must demonstrate need to be eligible for a subsidized Stafford Loan. Families without need may receive an unsubsidized Stafford.

What is Need? It's the cost of your college minus your expected family contribution (EFC) minus any aid (e.g., private scholarships) you bring to the college. Family contribution, to refresh your memory, is determined by a federally-approved formula called the "Federal Methodology" (see the appendices for the calculation), and is based on information you provide when you fill out the Free Application for Federal Student Aid (FAFSA).

What is Remaining Need? It's your calculated need, minus the value of any Pell Grant you receive. Let's run through some examples:

1. **The Shishka Family.** One Shishka, Bob, is starting at a two-year college. Annual cost: $9,000. The family was judged capable of contributing $4,000 to college costs which means they would have qualified for an $1,550 Pell Grant ($5,550 - $4,000). Earlier, young Shishka won a $1,000 scholarship in a recipe contest for his barbecue sauce. What's this family's remaining need?

    $9,000 - ($4,000 + $1,550 + $1,000) = $2,450

2. **The Knight Family.** Two children. Lance and Lot. Lance, the chivalrous one, goes to Gallahad State. Annual cost: $20,000. He receives a $5,000 scholarship. Lot, the gallant one, goes to Round Table U. Annual Cost: $6,000. He earns a $800 educational bonus from the National Guard. The Knight family contribution was judged to be $4,000 for each child. What's this family's remaining need?

> For Lance: $20,000 - ($5,000 + $4,000) or $11,000.
>
> For Lot: $6,000 - ($5,000 + $800) or $200.

3. **Donnie Dodge** is a graduate student at a $35,000 school. He has a family contribution of $8,000 and receives a $15,000 scholarship through the Challenger Program. What's his remaining need?

> $35,000 - ($8,000 + $15,000) or $12,000.

Even though it is authorized, don't think you'll get a $200 loan just because you have a need of $200. The cost of paper processing would make this highly unprofitable. In fact schools need not certify eligibility for loans under $200. Let's see how the students in our first two examples might have fared in their first year of college:

- Shishka Bob qualifies for an $2,450 subsidized Stafford and a $3,050 unsubsidized Stafford ($5,500 - $2,450) which he may use to help pay his $4,000 Expected Family Contribution.

- Lance Knight would be eligible for a $3,500 subsidized loan, and a $2,000 unsubsidized loan. His brother Lot would probably not be certified for a subsidized loan, but could borrow the full $5,500 under the unsubsidized Stafford.

Remember, these loan limits all increase after the freshman year!

- Now let's turn to Donnie Dodge. He has $12,000 in need, so, as a graduate student, he would be eligible for the maximum, $8,500 subsidized Stafford. How about the unsubsidized Stafford? This is a little trickier. His cost of attendance is $35,000. He received a $15,000 scholarship and a $8,500 subsidized loan, which leaves him eligible for a $11,500 unsubsidized loan ($35,000 - $15,000 - $8,500). The maximum unsubsidized loan is higher than this ($12,000), but a federal student loan may not exceed the cost of attendance minus financial aid received. Donnie may, however, use the unsubsidized loan to pay his EFC.

Will We Qualify for a Loan?

People always ask, "Will we qualify for a loan?" There is no easy answer. It depends on income, size of family, number of students in college at the same time, and the cost of attendance. The cost of attendance, remember, includes tuition, fees, room, board, books, transportation, and personal care expenses. It can even include the cost of a new computer. At our most expensive schools, this cost now exceeds $50,000.

Use the appendices to estimate your family contribution. Now, compare your family contribution to the cost of the college you plan to attend. If your family contribution is less than the cost of college, you have need and are eligible for a subsidized Stafford. If your family contribution is greater than the cost of college, you do not have need but are eligible for an unsubsidized Stafford, which has been discussed throughout this chapter.

Applying for Stafford Loans

The FAFSA doubles as a Stafford Loan application. It allows your school to determine the amount of subsidized and unsubsidized loans you are eligible to receive. Your school records this information on a "Master Promissory Note" (MPN). You fill in your name, address, date of birth, social security number, driver's license number, and two personal references. Finally, you sign the form and return it to your school. Uncle will then use this MPN to wire money directly to your school account.

Important: Even though unsubsidized Staffords are not based on financial need, you must file a FAFSA to be eligible.

When Should You Apply?

As soon as possible after choosing which college you will attend. Most students wait too long to get the process underway, creating application traffic jams. Our suggestion: Start in late spring. You want to make certain your loan money is in place before the tuition bill comes due.

Finding Lenders

All new loans are to be made under the government's Direct Lending Program so you no longer need to worry about finding a lender. The federal government will work with all accredited schools to originate federal student loans.

You and Your Loan

Under the Higher Education Act, some important information must be disclosed to you when the loan is made and when repayment begins:

- A statement (in big, bold print) that this is a loan that must be repaid.
- A loan repayment schedule, including the loan amount, the interest rate, length of the grace period, and when you must start repaying.
- The yearly and cumulative amounts that may be borrowed.
- An explanation of the effect of the loan on eligibility for other student assistance.

- An estimate of your total debt, your monthly payments, including the minimum annual payment required and the minimum and maximum repayment periods.
- A tally of special charges such as loan origination and insurance fees and information on how these are collected.
- An explanation of special options available to the borrower for loan consolidation or refinancing.
- A statement that you have the right to prepay without penalty.
- An explanation of forbearance and of all deferment and cancellation provisions, including a notice of the Department of Defense's repayment options (to encourage you to enlist in the military).
- A statement that loan information will be reported to a credit bureau.
- A definition of default and a lurid description of what happens to defaulters (you may augment this description by re-reading Virgil's observations on his descent into hell—see Dante's *Inferno*).

Entrance and Exit Counseling

Schools must provide entrance and exit counseling for their borrowers—often this is done on-line rather than in-person. Sessions should review:

- The terms and conditions of loan programs, including interest rates, fees, loan limits, repayment options, and repayment schedules.
- The obligation of loan repayment, including the consequences of delinquency and default.
- The provisions for forbearance, deferment, and cancellation.
- The lender's obligation to keep the student informed about changes in the loan's assignment, including name, address and phone number of the new lender and/or servicer.
- The student's obligation to keep the lender informed about changes in enrollment status, name, and address.

What happens if your school fails to provide you with these items of information? Can you sue for civil damages or refuse to abide by the terms of your loan? No, you can't, however, you can report the school to the Department of Education.

Deferments, Forbearance, and Cancellation

Deferments

Deferments are granted whenever a student is enrolled at least half-time. You need not borrow more money to qualify for this deferment, but you must be at a school that meets Stafford eligibility requirements. Deferments are also authorized for:

1. Up to 3 years if unemployed and eligible for unemployment benefits.
2. Up to 3 years if facing economic hardship (e.g., working full-time for minimum wage, or less).
3. Study in an approved graduate fellowship program or in a rehabilitation training program for the disabled.
4. Active-duty military (or National Guard) service during time of war, national emergency or other military operations.

Forbearance

If unanticipated problems affect your ability to repay the loan, and you do not qualify for deferment, the government may grant forbearance—permitting (1) the temporary cessation of payments, (2) an extension of time for making payments, or (3) smaller payments than were scheduled.

Typical reasons for forbearance: unemployment, poor health, personal problems or underemployment (you automatically qualify if your student loans exceed 20% of your gross income). You must also be granted forbearance if you're participating in a community or military service program with loan repayment incentives, or you're in a medical or dental internship or residency program. Finally, you must be granted forbearance (for up to 60 days) while changing repayment plans or completing the paperwork for loan consolidation.

Interest on the loan continues to accumulate during forbearance.

Cancellation

We hope none of you qualify for cancellation, which is only for death, and permanent total disability.

Repayment

Repayment begins after the first grace period or immediately after subsequent deferments and lasts from 5 to 10 years.

The minimum annual payment is $600.

Table 1 illustrates the 10-year repayment load on subsidized Staffords incurred by a borrower at 3.4% (the interest rate which will be in effect beginning July 1, 2011). You can estimate your monthly payments for loan amounts other than those listed by dividing the total loan by 101.61 (for 3.4% loans).

Table 2 illustrates the 10-year repayment load on unsubsidized Staffords incurred by a borrower at 6.8%. You can estimate your monthly payments for loan amounts other than those listed by dividing the total loan by 86.90

If one portion of your loan comes from the subsidized Stafford program, and another portion from the unsubsidized program, you can combine numbers from Tables 1 and 2 for a rough estimate of your loan burden. Or you can use a calculator like that found on the Sallie Mae website under "repaying student loans" (www.salliemae.com).

Table 1: Repayment Schedule for Subsidized Stafford Loans	
Loan Amount	Monthly / Total Payment (3.4%)
$10,000	$98.42 / $11,810.13
$23,000	$226.36 / $27,163.44
$65,500	$644.64 / $77,356.60
$XX	101.61

After increasing the maximum (subsidized plus unsubsidized) loan amount to $138,500 (see next page), Congress realized it must do something to lessen the repayment burden. For example, all lenders must offer a choice of regular or graduated repayment plans. For an explanation of your payment options and repayment schedules under federal loan consolidation, see Chapter 11.

Prepayment: Loans can be prepaid without penalty.

Table 2: Repayment Schedule for Unsubsidized Stafford Loans	
Loan Amount	Monthly / Total Payment (6.8%)
$8,000	$92.06 / $11,047.93
$31,000	$356.75 / $42,809.83
$34,500	$397.03 / $47,634.11
$57,500	$661.71 / $79,405.53
$73,000	$840.09 / $100,810.19
$138,500	$1593.86/ $191,263.64
$XX	86.90

Repayment by Uncle Sam

You can have your loan repaid by Uncle Sam:

1. For service in Americorps. Up to $5,550/year of service for up to two years.

2. For service as an enlisted member of the National Guard or Reserve: $1,500 or 15% of loan, whichever is greater, per year of service to a maximum of $10,000 (up to $20,000 in selected skills).

3. For service in the Regular Army: $1,500 or 33 1/3% of the loan, whichever is greater, per year of service to a maximum of $65,000.

In addition, there is a growing recognition that high debt levels affect career choices—the higher your debt, the less likely you are to work in a non-profit or public service field. So now:

1. Up to $5,000 in loans may be forgiven for teaching for five consecutive years in a "shortage area." Shortage areas may refer to a grade-level, subject area or geographic region—the definition varies by state. For a listing, go to www.ed.gov/offices/OSFAP/Students/repayment/teachers/stcol.html. This amount may be increased to $17,500 for those working in low-income areas teaching math, science or special ed.

2. A portion may also be forgiven for working in areas of "National Need" (as defined by Uncle Sam), for example, early childhood educators, child-welfare workers and medical specialists. Some federal agencies also forgive loans for their employees; the exact terms are up to the individual agencies.

3. Up to $6,000 per year (to a maximum of $40,000) for working as a civil legal assistance attorney.

4. The government now offers a "Public Service Loan Forgiveness Program" to forgive the balance of your loans if you have been repaying them for 10 years while working in a public service job (for example, law enforcement, social work, public health, or public education).

Gaining an Advantage

- Schools do not have to certify you for subsidized Staffords of less than $200. If you fall into this low-need category, think carefully about your family's financial situation, and if appropriate, discuss it with the financial aid administrator. Otherwise you'll have to make do with unsubsidized Stafford money.

- Repayment options can make your loan burden more manageable, but also more costly (due to longer repayment periods).

- You might receive extra bonuses (in the form of lower interest rates) if you repay your loans automatically via electronic bank transfers.

- Middle-income families may deduct interest payments on their education loans.

CHAPTER 7

■■■■■■■■■■■■■■■■■■■

FEDERAL PLUS LOANS

Historical Perspective

Once upon a time, Congress authorized a parent loan program which the Department of Education decided to call PLUS loans—Parent Loans to Undergraduate Students. Congress soon expanded the parent loan program to include independent undergraduates and graduate students. In making this move, Congress renamed the program "Auxiliary Loan Program to Assist Students." Within 24 hours of the law's passage, wits had discovered the new program could be abbreviated ALAS, an acronym that gave cynics a great opportunity to practice their specialty.

The Department of Education was not amused. It decided to ignore the official name of the program (ignoring what Congress directs often seems to be a specialty of the Department of Education) and went back to the PLUS acronym, even though the acronym didn't really stand for anything.

Program Summary

Previously, the PLUS loan was limited to the parents (or legal guardians) of dependent, undergraduate students who are enrolled at least half-time. Now graduate students are once again eligible for PLUS loans, however, they must first file a FAFSA and apply for a Stafford loan.

Loan Limits: You may borrow an amount up to the school's total cost of attendance minus other aid received. PLUS loans are not based on financial need, so you may use them to cover your expected family contribution. Many lenders won't make PLUS loans of less than $500 because these smaller amounts are not worth the paperwork.

Example: Ray Joseph attends an $10,500 college. He receives a $3,500 Stafford Loan and a $3,000 soccer scholarship. Remaining cost: $10,500 - ($3,500 + $3000) or $4,000. Ray's parents may borrow up to $4,000.

If parents cannot pass a credit check, they may secure an endorser who can. A student whose parent is still unable to secure a loan may borrow amounts up to the Independent Student limits proscribed in the unsubsidized Stafford program.

Interest Rate. The interest rate for PLUS loans is 7.9%..

Grace Period. None. Interest begins accruing when the loan is issued.

Origination and Insurance Fees: Uncle Sam deducts a 4% loan origination/insurance fee.

Lenders: Your loan comes straight from Uncle Sam.

What Information Must Be Disclosed: The same disclosures as for a Stafford Loan (see Chapter 6).

Eligible Schools: Accredited colleges and universities; eligible vocational, technical, trade, business and foreign schools.

Borrower Certifications: Borrowers must sign a certificate that the loan money will be used solely for defraying the cost of attendance at the school the student is or will be attending.

Applying for PLUS Loans

To apply for a PLUS loan, you must complete a simple application and pass a credit check. Parents (unlike graduate students) do not have to file a FAFSA (unless of course, your school says otherwise). Your school's aid administrator will certify your eligibility for a PLUS and ask Uncle to wire money directly to your school account. Simply answer a few credit-related questions and you'll learn within minutes if you're approved.

Repayment

Repayment begins 60 days after the final loan disbursement for the academic year and extends from 5 to 10 years. Parent and student borrowers have the option to defer payment until six months after the student ceases to be enrolled at least half-time, however, interest continues to accrue.

Tip: As with unsubsidized Stafford loans, don't let the interest capitalize; instead, pay the interest while you're in school. The charges are minimal, and you'll save hundreds of dollars during repayment. Also, if your income is below the caps described in Chapter 10, you can deduct the interest payments from your AGI saving you tax dollars as well.

Parents must be given the option of standard or graduated repayment; in some case, they may be given the choice of extended repayment plans, as well. (see Chapter 10)

Minimum Annual Repayment: $600.

Prepayment: Loans can be prepaid without penalty.

Deferments, Forbearance, and Cancellations

Under certain circumstances, loans can be deferred, postponed, canceled or considered for forbearance. Usually these circumstances are unpleasant things like death, permanent disability, or economic hardship.

Interest continues to accrue during forbearance and deferments.

Uncle will repay a portion of your parents' PLUS loan if you (the student) serve in the Army, Army Reserves, Army National Guard or Air National Guard (again, see Chapter 6). There are no other forgiveness features.

Table 3: 10-Year Repayment Schedule for PLUS Loans	
Loan Amount	**120 Monthly Payments (7.9%)**
$5,000	$60
12,000	145
30,000	362
50,000	604
80,000	966
$ XXX	82.82

You can estimate your monthly payments for loan amounts other than those listed above by dividing the total loan by 82.82.

CHAPTER 8

■■■■■■■■■■■■■■■■■■■■■

FEDERAL PERKINS LOANS

Program Summary

Federal Perkins Loans are awarded to students with demonstrated financial need. Funds for the program are allocated to schools by Uncle Sam. Schools select the recipients and specify the loan amounts. Money is available to both undergraduate and graduate students. The average award is around $2,200.

Loan Limits:

Undergraduate: $5,500 per year to a maximum of $27,500.

Graduate students: $8,000 per year to a maximum of $60,000 (less any Perkins money borrowed as an undergraduate).

Interest Rate:

5%. Student does not pay interest while in school, during deferments, or during grace periods.

Deferments:

Deferments are authorized for:

- Students pursuing at least a half-time course of study as determined by an eligible institution.
- Students pursuing a course of study pursuant to a graduate fellowship program or rehabilitation training program for disabled individuals (this deferment does not include medical internships or residencies).
- Students engaged in services which qualify them for loan forgiveness (see below).
- Active-duty military (or National Guard) service during time of war, national emergency or other military operations.
- Up to three years if unemployed, and eligible to receive unemployment benefits (e.g., actively searching for full-time employment).
- Up to three years if facing economic hardship (e.g., working full-time at less than minimum wage).

Question: How do I get approved for one of these deferments?

Answer: Contact the school's student loan officer *before* your first payment is due and complete the paperwork he or she sends you. Simple.

Loan Cancellation:

Loan cancellation is available to:

- Full-time teachers in pre-schools, elementary or secondary schools serving handicapped students or low-income families.
- Full-time special education teachers or professional providers of early intervention services to children with disabilities.
- Full-time law enforcement or correction officers.
- Full-time teachers of math, science, foreign languages, bilingual education, or any other subject in which the state educational agency determines a "shortage."
- Full-time nurses or medical technicians providing health care services.
- Full-time employees of child or family service agencies providing services to high-risk, low-income children and their families.

The cancellation rate for each of the above: 15% for each of the first two years; 20% for each of the third and fourth years; and 30% in the fifth year.

- People serving in the Armed Forces if they are stationed in "an area of hostilities." *Cancellation Rate*: 12.5% per year of service to a maximum of 50%.
- People serving as Peace Corps or ACTION volunteers. *Cancellation Rate*: 15% for each of the first two years of service; 20% for each of the third and fourth years to a maximum of 70%.
- Full-time staff member employed in a professional capacity as part of a Head Start program. *Cancellation Rate:* 15% per year of service.

You might also be eligible to have your loan canceled if you are a full-time faculty member at a Tribal College or University; full-time librarian at a low-income school; full-time speech pathologist (with a masters degree) working exclusively at a low income school; or a firefighter.

Forbearance: Institutions must grant students forbearance for up to three years under special circumstances, for example, if the borrower's student loan debt burden equals or exceeds 20% of his or her gross income. Interest continues to accrue.

Repayment by Uncle Sam:

- For service as an enlisted member of the Army National Guard or Reserve: $1,500 or 15% of the loan, whichever is greater, per year of service to a maximum of $10,000 (or $20,000 in selected skills).
- For service as an enlisted member in the Army: $1,500 or 33 1/3% of the loan, whichever is greater, to a maximum of $65,000.

Outright Cancellation: We hope no one qualifies for outright cancellation, which is available only for death and permanent, total disability.

Grace Periods: Nine months after the student drops below half-time and six months after every deferment (except hardship deferments).

Repayment: Begins nine months after completing studies and extends over ten years (not including deferments and grace periods). Borrowers may now repay their loans using electronic bank transfers.

Minimum Annual Repayment: $480/year.

On the Horizon. The Administration wants to greatly expand the Perkins Program so that 3 million students would share an additional $5 billion. To help fund this increase, the Administration would raise the interest rate to 6.8% and eliminate the in-school interest subsidy.

Table 4: Repayment Schedule for Perkins Loans

Loan Amount	Monthly Payment	Number of Months	Total Interest	Total Payment
$5,500	58.34	120	1500.18	7,000.18
8,000	84.85	120	2,182.38	10,182.38
16,000	169.70	120	4,364.75	20,364.75
22,000	233.34	120	6,001.44	28,001.44
27,500	291.68	120	7,501.63	35,001.63
60,000	636.39	120	16,367.28	76,367.28

You can estimate your monthly payments for loan amounts other than those listed above by dividing the total loan by 94.28.

Finding Perkins Money

Perkins Loans are a tremendous deal. But Perkins money is not evenly distributed. Most of it is allocated to four-year colleges (public and private). And even within this group, some have plenty of Perkins money and some may not have enough to put together one loan. Why this disparity? Loan collection practices. Colleges which are too lax about collecting past loans have no new funds to distribute. Colleges that go after their borrowers, however, have plenty of money being returned to the revolving fund and Uncle Sam rewards their diligence by adding extra shots of new capital.

Uncle adds up to $300 million in new capital each year, otherwise schools must make due with the $1 billion "revolving fund" (money paid back by borrowers each year).

Our advice: Ask schools about their Perkins default rate. A high rate means no low-interest money, and possibly a school full of people who are so selfish they cheat future students out of loan money. A low rate points to more generous loans, a more conscientious group of students, and more efficient administrators.

CHAPTER 9
■ ■ ■ ■ ■ ■ ■ ■ ■ ■ ■ ■ ■ ■ ■ ■ ■ ■ ■ ■

LOANS AND GRANTS
FOR MEDICAL TRAINING

Bureau of Health Professions

The federal government spends lots of money—almost a half billion dollars per year—to educate future doctors, nurses, and other health professions. Most of this money is given directly to the schools; schools then select the recipients.

One bit of advice: You will gain an advantage over fellow applicants if you indicate a willingness to practice in a "shortage area." Don't worry about what a shortage area is. Its definition and location will change several times between the time you apply and the time you graduate. What's important to know is that "shortage areas" are a big thing at the Department of Health & Human Services. It has "primary medical care shortage areas," "dental manpower shortage areas," "rural dental shortage areas," "vision care shortage areas," "podiatry shortage areas," "pharmacy shortage areas," "psychiatric shortage areas," even "veterinary care shortage areas."

The nursing shortage is especially acute, which is why there are expanded grants and loan repayment options for nursing education.

For more information on all of the individual-based health care programs listed below contact the Health Resources and Services Administration, 800/221-9393, callcenter@hrsa.gov, www.hrsa.gov/loanscholarships.

For example:

Health Professions Student Loans (HPSL)

Long-term, low-interest, need-based loans for students in dentistry, optometry, pharmacy, podiatry or veterinary medicine. Must practice in primary care. Apply through school.

Primary Care Loans (PCL)

Students in allopathic or osteopathic medicine may borrow up to the cost of attendance. Interest equals 5% and begins to accrue following a one-year grace period after you cease to be a full-time student. Deferment options of up to four years. Must practice in primary health care until the loan is repaid. Apply through school, bhpr.hrsa.gov/dsa/pcl.htm.

Nursing Student Loans

When money is available, these need-based loans go to half- and full-time students pursuing study at schools of professional nursing. Apply through your school's financial aid office.

Nursing Scholarship Program

Tuition, fees and monthly stipend of c. $1,325. Priority goes to those with a "zero" EFC (from the FAFSA), very competitive. Must practice for at least 2 years at a health care facility with a critical shortage of nurses. By late June, 877/464-4772, bhpr.hrsa.gov/nursing/scholarship.

Nursing Education Loan Repayment Program (NELRP)

Helps nurses repay educational loans in exchange for service in eligible facilities located in areas experiencing a shortage of nurses. For two years of service, the NELRP will pay 60% of the participant's loan balance; for a third year of service, NELRP will pay an additional 25% of the loan balance. By early-March. Nurse Education Loan Repayment Program, 877/464-4772, bhpr.hrsa.gov/nursing/loanrepay.htm.

Scholarships and Loans for Disadvantaged Students (SDS and LDS Programs)

Scholarships and low-interest loans for full-time, financially needy students from disadvantaged backgrounds who are enrolled in health professional and nursing programs. Apply through school.

Exceptional Financial Need Scholarships

All tuition plus stipend. Good for one year only. At year's end, participants have priority for a NHSC Scholarship (see below). Must practice in general dentistry or primary care medicine for five years after residency. Apply through school.

National Institutes of Health

Medical researchers at NIH can qualify for up to $35,000 in loan forgiveness, and an extra amount to cover federal and state income taxes that result from these repayments, 866/849-4047, lrp.info.nih.gov.

National Health Service Corps

The National Health Service Corps is a $145 million program operated by the Health Resources and Services Administration (HRSA). It recruits and places primary care specialists (physicians, nurses, dentists, dental hygienists and physician assistants) throughout medically underserved communities in the U.S. Eligible students may receive a full tuition (plus stipend) scholarships or participate in a loan repayment program. For more information, contact: National Health Service Corps, nhsc.bhpr.hrsa.gov.

National Health Service Corps Scholarship Program

The NHSC will pay tuition, fees, books and supplies, plus stipend (nearly $1,300 per month) for up to four years. This very-competitive program is open to US citizens enrolled in a fully-accredited medical school, dental school, family nurse practitioner program, nurse midwifery program or physician assistant program. For each year of support, you owe one year of full-time clinical practice in high-priority health professions shortage areas. Minimum 2 year obligation. If you fail to comply with the terms of your contract, the penalty equals three times the cost of your scholarship, plus interest. The scholarship is tax exempt; the stipend remains taxable. NHSC Scholarship Program, 800/638-0824, nhsc.bhpr.hrsa.gov.

National Health Service Corps Loan Repayment Program

In exchange for providing primary care in federally-designated health profession shortage areas, the program will repay up to $60,000 in education loans for a minimum 2-year commitment. The program is open to primary care physicians (family medicine, OB/gyn, internal medicine, pediatrics, general psychiatry), mental health care clinicians (psychiatrists, psychologists, family counselors and clinical social workers), nurse practitioners, midwives, dentists, dental hygienists and physician assistants. By late March. NHSC Loan Repayment Program, 800/638-0824, nhsc.bhpr.hrsa.gov.

Faculty Loan Repayment Program

Helps eligible health-professions faculty from disadvantaged backgrounds repay their student loans. Up to $20,000 per year in exchange for a two-year service commitment, bhpr.hrsa.gov/dsa/flrp.

State-Based Programs

Many states have loan repayment programs (some of which are funded by the National Health Service Corps, nhsc.bhpr.hrsa.gov). For a listing, check out the financial aid section of the American Medical Colleges web site, www.aamc.org/students/financing/start.htm.

Military Medical and Nursing Programs

Armed Forces Health Professional Programs

Health Professions Scholarships for medical, dental, veterinary, psychiatric nurse practitioner, optometry and psychology students. Tuition, fees and monthly stipend of more than $2,000 (adjusted each July). Additional sign-on bonus for certain medical and dental students of up to $20,000. Service obligation of one year for each year you receive the scholarship.

Health Professional Loan Repayment Program (HPLRP). Depending on branch of service, up to $40,000 per year in educational loans for officers serving up to three years on active duty in designated specialties

Financial Assistance Program. Residency training for graduate physicians, endodontists, periodontists, orthodontists and oral surgeons. $45,000 per year for up to four years plus $2,000+ monthly stipend (adjusted each July). Service obligation.

Each branch of the service has its own point of contact:

- **Army:** Medical Department, 800/USA-ARMY, www.goarmy.com/amedd/index.jsp.
- **Navy:** Medical Command, 301/319-4118, www.navy.com/healthcareopportunities.
- **Air Force:** Dir. of Health Professionals, 800/443-4690, www.airforce.com/opportunities/healthcare/education.

ROTC Nurse Program (Army, Navy, Air Force)

Students at approved nursing schools affiliated with an Army, Navy, or Air Force ROTC unit. 2, 3, 4 year scholarships; tuition, textbooks, and fees, plus a monthly stipend. Service obligation.

- **Army,** Army ROTC, www.goarmy.com/rotc/nurse_program.jsp.
- **Navy,** 800/NAV-ROTC, www.nrotc.navy.mil.
- **Air Force,** HQ AFROTC, 866/423-7682, www.afrotc.com.

Navy-Specific Programs

For more information on the following programs, contact the Navy Medical Command, 301/319-4118, www.navy.com/healthcareopportunities.

1. *Navy Health Services Collegiate Program.* Up to $240,000 to finish graduate school in the form of a monthly salary and housing allowance.
2. *Navy Nurse Candidate Program.* $10,000 upfront plus $1,000 per month for 24 months for nursing school.

AArmy-Specific Programs

HQ, US Army Recruiting Command, Health Services Division, 1307 Third Avenue, Fort Knox, KY 40121, 800/USA-ARMY, www.goarmy.com/amedd.html

1. *Specialized Training Assistance Program (STRAP).* Monthly stipend for students and residents in designated specialties including nursing (specialties are identified every two years). $2,000+/month (adjusted each July). Recipients serve one year in the Reserve component of the Army Medical Department for every six months (or less) they receive the stipend.
2. *Health Professional Loan Repayment Program (HPLRP).* Army will repay up to $50,000 in educational loans for officers serving in designated specialties in the Reserves—$20,000 in each of the first two years, and $10,000 in the third year.

3. *Health Professions Special Pay.* Annual bonus of up to $20,000 for three years to health care professionals in designated specialties (specialties are identified every two years) who join the Army Reserve. Also, Active Duty bonus from $2,000 to $5,000 per year, depending on the specialty.

4. *Army Nurse Candidate Program.* Bonus money for undergraduates pursuing nursing degrees: $5,000 when entering the program, another $5,000 at graduation, plus $1,000 per month during enrollment.

Uniformed Services University of the Health Sciences

Fully-accredited federal school of medicine and graduate school of nursing. Request catalogue, from Admissions Office, 4301 Jones Bridge Rd., Bethesda, MD 20814; 800/772-1743, www.usuhs.mil.

F. Edward Hebert School of Medicine. This tuition-free institution's main emphasis is on training medical officers for the Army, Navy and Air Force. While enrolled, students serve on active duty as Reserve commissioned officers in grade O-1 with full pay and allowances. Civilian and uniformed services personnel are eligible for admission. Seven year service obligation, exclusive of internship, residency or other service obligations.

Graduate School of Nursing. Offers degrees in Nurse Anesthesia, Psychiatric Mental Health Nurse Practitioner, Family Nurse Practitioner and Perioperative Clinical Nurse Specialist as well as a Ph.D. in Nursing Science.

Commissioned Officer Student Training & Extern Program Work Program (COSTEP)

For graduate awards, students must complete one year of medical, dental, veterinary school. For undergrad awards, students must complete two years in a dietary, nursing, pharmacy, dental hygiene, medical laboratory technology, therapy, sanitary science, medical records, engineering, physician's assistant, or computer science field. Student must return to studies following completion of COSTEP assignment. Serve as an extern in various divisions of the US Department of Health and Human Services during school breaks of 31-120 days duration. Ensign's pay during work phases, about $2,500 per month. COSTEP, 800/279-1605, www.usphs.gov/student.

Office of Minority Health Resource Center.

A central resource for minorities interested in the health professions. The Resource Center does not offer scholarships, but its trained information specialists will be glad to help you search its database of funding opportunities—via the Web, www.omhrc.gov or phone, 800/444-6472.

CHAPTER 10
■■■■■■■■■■■■■■■■■■■■

IT'S PAYBACK TIME

The plans outlined in this chapter will give you a general overview of your loan repayment options. Exact details vary depending on the nature of your debt. Besides, by the time you begin repayment, all of these choices will probably be obsolete! For current information, contact the institution that gave you your loan.

Alternate Loan Repayment Options

Borrowers who face larger payments than they can initially handle under regular repayment, may want to use an alternate plan, either Extended Repayment, Graduated Repayment, or an Income-Based Repayment. Borrowers may also consolidate their loans and take advantage of extended repayment plans.

Table 5: Repayment Options for a $23,000 Subsidized Stafford Loan		
	Stafford Loan	**Consolidation Loan**
Standard Repayment **Total Payments**	$255, 120 months **$30,642**	$164.78, 240 months **$39,547**
Graduated Repayment	$115, 24 months $302, 96 months	$115 initial payment increasing to $263 final payment (after 20 years)
Total Payments	**$31,776**	**$43,281**

By letting you take longer for repayment, Uncle is not reducing your debt, just the size of your payments (anywhere from 6-35%, depending on the size of your loan). Without these options, your first paycheck, your second paycheck, even your one hundred and twentieth paycheck could be consumed by taxes, bus fare, burgers and student loan payments. With longer repayment plans, paychecks can go toward an occasional candlelight dinner at Chez Froggy or a spring trip to the Amalfi coast. But please note, under all of these plans, your monthly payments will be smaller but the total amount you repay much greater than under standard (10-year) repayment.

Uncle currently runs two parallel sets of repayment plans, one under Federal Family Education Loan (FFEL), the other under Federal Direct Student Loan (FDSL). Since FFEL is being phased out, students are being offered incentives (in the form of loan reductions) to switch over to the Direct Loan program (to speed the elimination of FFEL). For more information, check with Uncle Sam or the institution that gave you your loan.

To help you decide which repayment plan is best for you, try using *FinAid's* online loan calculators: www.finaid.org/calculators.

- If the student is repaying Stafford loans only, the interest rate is 4.5% for subsidized amounts, and 6.8% for unsubsidized amounts.
- If the family is repaying PLUS only, the interest rate is either 7.9% (FDSL) or 8.5% (FFEL).
- If the student is repaying a consolidated loan, the interest rate equals the weighted average of all the consolidated loans rounded up to the nearest 1/8% with an 8.25% cap.

Table 5 shows the options for repaying a $23,000 subsidized Stafford. No matter what the interest rate (we've used 6%), total payments are lowest under standard repayment.

Standard Repayment

Unless borrowers make other arrangements, they must repay their loans in equal installments, spread over ten years. We included sample repayment charts in previous chapters.

Graduated Repayment

Borrowers must repay the loan within ten years, however, payments start small when income is low, and increase over time, while income also rises. Students sometimes have the option of making interest-only payments for the first few years.

Extended Repayment

Students with debts over $30,000 may extend repayment for up to 25 years and choose between a fixed or graduated repayment schedule.

Income-Based Repayment

All students may now take advantage of a new, income-based repayment. In this plan, a student's monthly loan payment will be limited to 15% of his or her discretionary income, defined as 15% of the amount by which the student's adjusted gross income exceeds 150% of the poverty line, divided by 12. Got it? The government will forgive any remaining balance after 25 years of repayment.

Borrowers who are using one of the other repayment plans may switch to this one. PLUS loans made to parents are not eligible for income-based repayment.

For more information, visit IBRInfo.org.

Table 6: Sample Maximum Monthly Payments under IBR				
	Family Size			
Income	**1**	**2**	**3**	**4**
$10,000	$0	$0	$0	$0
$20,000	$47	$0	$0	$0
$30,000	$172	$102	$32	$0
$40,000	$297	$227	$157	$87
$50,000	$422	$352	$282	$212

Loan Consolidation

Loan consolidation is another option, especially for students with multiple loans who are trying to simplify repayment. You may consolidate all federal loans—Stafford, Perkins, PLUS, Nursing, Loans for Disadvantaged Students and Health Profession Student Loans—and take advantage of the repayment plans just described. Married couples may no longer consolidate their individual loans into a joint loan.

For more on FFEL Consolidation, contact your current lender. For more on Direct Consolidation, visit www.loanconsolidation.ed.gov.

Sample Repayment Periods:
- 10 years for loans under $7,500;
- 12 years for loans between $7,500 and $9,999;
- 15 years for loans between $10,000 and $19,999;
- 20 years for loans between $20,000 and $39,999;
- 25 years for loans between $40,000 and $59,999; and
- 30 years for those lucky students with more than $60,000 to repay.

Interest Rate. The interest rate equals the weighted average of all your loans rounded up to the nearest 1/8% with an 8.25% cap. It is fixed at this rate for the life of the loan.

Interest Subsidies. If your consolidation loan contains subsidized loan money, you might retain the interest subsidy benefit on that portion of your consolidated loan during deferments.

Deferment: Deferment periods are not included in the number of years allowed for repayment. Also, *if you choose to consolidate a Perkins or Stafford loan, you could lose out on their deferment and forgiveness options, so read the rules carefully before your sign up..* Deferment is allowed:

1. While in school at least half-time;
2. While pursuing a graduate fellowship program or rehabilitation training program for persons with disabilities;
3. Up to three years for unemployment or economic hardship; and
4. Up to three years for active-duty military service.

Loan Forgiveness: Consolidation loans are eligible for the Public Service Loan Forgiveness program described in Chapter 6.

Deduction for Student Loan Interest

You may deduct up to $2,500 per year in interest paid on "qualified education loans." This definition includes commercial education loans, but not loans from people related to the taxpayer. The deduction will be phased out for single filers with incomes between $60,000 and $75,000 and joint filers with incomes between $120,000 and $150,000. Income levels will be indexed annually for inflation.

Plan Now, Save Later

Borrower Bonuses

Students who repay their loans faithfully sometimes receive a bonus, for example, the interest rate could be lowered by 2% after receiving 48 on-time payments, or .25% for using automatic electronic payments. To benefit from these opportunities, set up overdraft protection on your checking account so you're sure not to miss a payment due to "insufficient funds."

CHAPTER 11

■■■■■■■■■■■■■■■■■■■■■■■■■

WAIT, THERE'S MORE
(ADDITIONAL SOURCES OF
FEDERAL ASSISTANCE)

AmeriCorps (AmeriCorps.gov)

Participants receive a minimum wage stipend plus an annual education award for each year of full-time service (for up to two years). They may use the credit at any college or graduate school, or to pay down outstanding student loans. Furthermore, the money does not affect eligibility for other federal student aid. Previously the credit was $4,725 per year. In 2010, it increased to $5,550 per year and will be tied in value to the maximum Pell.

Currently, about 50,000 students serve in 450 different programs with Uncle providing most of the funding, but states and nonprofits doing the hiring. Prime projects are those that address unmet needs in education (assisting teachers in Head Start), the environment (recycling or conservation projects), human services (building housing for the homeless) or public safety (leading drug education seminars).

The new Edward M. Kennedy Serve America Act reauthorizes and expands national service programs, increasing the number of AmeriCorps positions to 250,000 by 2017 and introducing two new programs. In both of these new programs, recipients must use their awards within ten years.

1. **Summer of Service.** $500 education awards for 6-12th graders who perform 100 hours of service. ($750 for economically-disadvantaged students). Students may earn two of these awards.

2. **Silver Scholar.** $1,000 education awards for volunteers age 55 and older who perform 350 hours of service. Silver Scholar awards may be transferred to a child or grandchild.

While AmeriCorps is small in scope, its real importance has been to focus attention on our county's extensive network of service programs. With AmeriCorps adding new structure, and a solid core of workers, these programs have become a magnet for corporate money as well as for volunteers with only an hour to spare. The funded projects have brought huge economic benefits to the communities in which they operate as well as a heightened sense of personal and social responsibility for the AmeriCorps participants.

Interested students should apply directly to a funded program (for a list, visit www.AmeriCorps.gov, 800/94-ACORPS).

Campus-Based Aid Programs

Uncle funds several additional programs—Supplemental Educational Opportunity Grants, Work-Study and TEACH grants—that are campus-based. This means Uncle provides money for the programs, but gives it to the colleges to dispense in accordance with federal guidelines. Most of the money goes to full- and half-time students, however, a small sum will go to part-time students.

Supplemental Educational Opportunity Grants (SEOG)

Uncle will give the colleges $757 million for SEOGs next year. Colleges must match 25% of this money with funds of their own.

Size of awards. From $100 to $4,000 per year of undergraduate study. Nearly 1.4 million undergraduates receive average grants of $716.

Criteria for Selection. Need and fund availability. Be smart. Apply early. Priority goes to those receiving Pells.

Work-Study

Uncle will give colleges over $1 billion for work-study next year. Colleges are supposed to match some of this money with funds of their own.

Eligibility. Undergraduate and graduate students. Over 713,000 students receive an average of $1,640 each.

Criteria for Selection. Need and fund availability. Be smart. Apply early.

Program Description. On- and off-campus employment. Salary must at least equal minimum wage. You cannot earn more than your award stipulates. Thus, if you receive a $1,000 award, your employment lasts until you earn $1,000 and then it terminates for that academic year. Schools are encouraged to use some of this money to fund community service jobs, including projects that will prepare communities to cope with emergencies and natural disasters. Employment may not involve political or religious activity nor may students be used to replace regular employees.

TEACH Grants

Teacher Education Assistance for College and Higher Education (TEACH) Grants will award up to $4,000 per year (to a maximum of $16,000 for under-graduates and $8,000 for graduate students) to students completing the coursework necessary to begin a career in teaching.

You begin the process of applying for a TEACH Grant by indicating your interest in teaching when you complete the FAFSA. Like the other campus-based programs, the federal government gives money to the colleges to dispense. Next year, $131 million will be awarded to 44,000 recipients, for an average award of $3,000.

Recipients must have at least a 3.25 GPA and agree to serve as a full-time teacher for at least four years in a high-need school within eight years of completing their course of study. Furthermore, they must teach Math,

Science, Foreign Language, Special Ed, or some other subject deemed "high need" by the federal, state or local government. Students who do not fulfill their obligation must repay their TEACH Grant with interest as though it was an unsubsidized Stafford.

■ ■ ■ ■ ■ ■ ■ ■ ■ ■ ■ ■ ■ ■ ■ ■ ■ ■

TAX RELIEF FOR
EDUCATION EXPENSES

Education can be the "Continental Divide" between those who will prosper economically and those who will not. Unfortunately, many families feel priced out of college, hence, the push to make middle-income tuition-payers the big tax-relief winners.

For more details on all types of education-related tax benefits, read the official IRS publications. In reviewing these sites, remember they are valuable for their factual information, not their consumer insights:

1. *Tax Information for Students* at www.irs.gov/individuals/students/index.html; or

2. *Tax Benefits for Education* at www.irs.gov/pub/irs-pdf/p970.pdf

American Opportunity Tax Credit (Formerly The Hope Credit)

The American Opportunity Credit allows taxpayers to claim a maximum annual credit of $2,500 per student for tuition and coursework expenses paid on behalf of the taxpayer, the taxpayer's spouse, or a dependent for the first four years of college; 100% of the first $2,000 of tuition, and 25% of the next $2,000. Families who do not pay taxes would be eligible for a refund of up to 40% of the maximum credit, or $1,000. To qualify, the student must be enrolled at least half-time.

This credit was introduced for 2009 and has been extended through 2012.

It will be phased out for single filers with adjusted gross incomes between $80,000 and $90,000, and joint filers with incomes between $160,000 and $180,000.

The Lifetime Learning Credit

The Lifetime Learning Credit allows taxpayers to claim an annual credit equal to 20% of up to $10,000 in total tuition expenses. Unlike the American Opportunity credit, this is a "per taxpayer" maximum, rather than a "per student" maximum. Also, part-timers are eligible, so are working-adults taking classes to improve their job skills. You need not be enrolled in a degree program to benefit, nor is there a limit to the number of years you may claim the credit. So, if you claim the American Opportunity Credit for one student for four years, and that student is taking a fifth year to finish his or her degree, you can use the Lifetime Learning Credit for expenses paid in that fifth year.

This credit will be phased out for single filers with adjusted gross incomes between $50,000 and $60,000, and joint filers with incomes between $100,000 and $120,000. Income levels are indexed annually for inflation.

Restrictions

You can only use one of these credits per student, per year, however, you can claim the American Opportunity Credit for one student's expenses and the Lifetime Learning Credit for another's. So, parents with incomes under $100,000 could use the American Opportunity credit for their full-time college student, and the Lifetime Learning credit for a second student, enrolled part-time, for a maximum total credit of $4,500.

If your family's income is too high to claim these credits, consider letting your child claim them on his or her tax return. This is possible only if the parents forego claiming that child on their return—you'll have to evaluate the benefit for yourself, however, in most instances, if the student has sufficient taxable income, the value of the tax credit outweighs the dependency exemption.

To claim your credit, simply file IRS Form 8863 with the rest of your 1040 tax return. Note: The FAFSA collects data on the size of your tuition credits, and the Federal Methodology provides offsets for them. Otherwise, these credits would increase available income, which would increase EFC, and decrease eligibility for aid...certainly not the tax writers' intent.

(Temporary) Deduction for Higher Education Expenses

Itemizers and non-itemizers alike with incomes under $130,000 ($65,000 for single filers) can deduct up to $4,000 per year in tuition expenses from their AGIs; families with incomes between $130,000 and $160,000 (or singles with incomes between $65,000 and $80,000) can deduct $2,000.

You may not deduct higher education expenses for a student in the same year you claim an American Opportunity or Lifetime Learning credit for that student. (Besides, the tax credits usually result in greater tax savings than this tax deduction.) In previous years, this deduction has been allowed to expire, and extended at the last minute.

Deduction for Student Loan Interest

You may deduct up to $2,500 per year in interest paid on "qualified education loans." This definition includes federal student loans as well as commercial education loans, but not loans from people related to the taxpayer. The deduction will be phased out for single filers with incomes between $60,000 and $75,000 and joint filers with incomes between $120,000 and $150,000. Income levels will be indexed for inflation.

APPENDIX
· · · · · · · · · · · · · · · · ·

DETERMINING ELIGIBILITY
ENHANCING ELIGIBILITY
RETAINING ELIGIBILITY

Student Assets

Student assets are assessed at a higher rate than parental assets (20% versus 5.6%). If a family can choose between leaving junior's assets in junior's own bank account or maintaining them in the parents' account, opt for the parental account. For example, the Lay family has an Expected Family Contribution of $10,000. State U. Costs $11,000, making them eligible for $1,000 in need-based aid (most likely, a subsidized loan). Daughter Frieda keeps $3,500 in her bank account. That sum, all by itself, chips in $700 of the family's EFC. If the Lays closed out Frieda's account (with her approval, of course) and added the money to the family account, the EFC would drop to $9,496 ($9,500 with rounding). The family is now eligible for $1,500 in need-based aid.

Of course, the family could also use Frieda's $3,500 to buy her a new laptop (or tablet) computer, printer, and other essential back-to-school gadgets. Then, the EFC drops to $9,300.

Student Income

Fifty percent of a student's after-tax income (over $5,250) counts towards student aid eligibility. So, encourage your student to work, especially if he or she can find a good summer job. But keep an eye on the total amount earned. If possible, students might be able to spend less time flipping burgers during the school year, and more time doing interesting volunteer work. Reducing their student's income from $6,000 to $5,500 can lower EFC by $250.

Retaining Your Eligibility

Students must make "satisfactory academic progress" to continue receiving federal aid. Usually this means at least a "C" average or academic standing consistent with the school's requirements for graduation. Some students lose eligibility because they didn't realize the academic pace in college is faster than in high school. They overloaded themselves with courses and flunked them all. Don't let this happen to you. If you are not sure of your ability to handle college-level work, test the water before plunging in. You'll be a lot happier, and a lot richer.

■■■■■■■■■■■■■■■■■

DEPENDENT STUDENTS
(2011/2012 ACADEMIC YEAR)

Parent's Contribution from Income

1. Parents' Adjusted Gross Income .... $_____
2. Parents' Tax-exempt Interest Income .... $_____
3. Veteran's Non-educational Benefits .... $_____
4. Parents' Other Untaxed Income and Benefits.
    This may include child support received,untaxed portions of pensions and
    IRA distributions, workers' compensation, disability payments, housing,
    food and living allowances for military, clergy or others .... $_____
5. Deductible IRA, Keogh, SEP, 403 (b), 401(k) pymnts made by parents ... $_____
6. **Total Income.** Add Lines 1 through 5 .... $_____
7. US Income Taxes paid .... $_____
8. State Income Taxes paid .... $_____
9. Social Security/Medicare Taxes paid .... $_____
10. Child Support paid by you for another child .... $_____
11. American Opportunity and/or Lifetime Learning credit, AmeriCorps awards,
    taxable earnings from Federal Work-Study (or other need-based work program)
    and other student financial aid that may have been included in Line 6. .... $_____
12. Income Protection Allowance from Table A .... $_____
13. Employment Expense Allowance. If both parents work, enter 35% of
    the lower income or $3,500, whichever is less. If your family has a
    single head of household, enter 35% of that income or $3,500, whichever
    is less. Otherwise, enter $0 .... $_____
14. **Total Allowances.** Add Lines 7 through 13 .... $_____
15. **Parents' Available Income.** Line 6 minus Line 14. If negative, subtract
    from Line 30 .... $_____

Parents Contribution from Assets[1]

16. Cash, savings and checking accounts .... $_____
17. Net Worth of real estate (excluding primary residence), investments, stocks,
    CDs, bonds, trusts, commodities, precious metals, college savings plans . $_____
18. Business and/or Commercial Farm Net Worth (excluding family farms
    and family-controlled small businesses) from Table B .... $_____
19. **Total Assets.** Add Lines 16 through 18 .... $_____
20. Asset Protection Allowance. From Table C .... $_____
21. Discretionary Net Worth. Line 19 minus Line 20 .... $_____
22. **CONTRIBUTION FROM ASSETS.** Multiply Line 21 by 12%.
    If negative, enter $0 .... $_____

Parental Contribution

23. Adjusted Available Income. Add Lines 15 and 22 .... $_____
24. **PARENT CONTRIBUTION.** From Table D. If negative, enter 0. .... $_____
25. Number in College Adjustment. Divide Line 24 by the number in college at
    least half-time (excluding parents). Quotient is the contribution/student .. $_____

Student's Contribution from Income

26. Student's Adjusted Gross Income .... $_____
27. Student's Tax-exempt Interest Income .... $_____
28. Student's Other Untaxed income and benefits. See Line 4.
    Also include any cash support paid on your behalf which was not
    reported elsewhere .... $_____
29. Deductible IRA payments made by student .... $_____
30. Total Income. Add lines 26 through 29 .... $_____
31. US Income Taxes paid .... $_____
32. State Income Taxes paid .... $_____
33. Social Security/Medicare Taxes paid .... $_____
34. AmeriCorps awards, student financial aid that may have been included
    in Line 30, taxable earnings from Federal Work-Study or other
    need-based work programs .... $_____
35. Income Protection Allowance. Enter $5,250 .... $_____
36. Total Allowances. Add Lines 31 through 35 .... $_____
37. Students Available Income. Line 30 minus Line 36 .... $_____
38. **STUDENT'S CONTRIBUTION FROM INCOME**
    Multiply Line 37 by 50%. If negative, enter $0 .... $_____

Student's Contribution from Assets[1]

39. Add net worth of all of student's assets—cash, savings, trusts,
    investments, real estate .... $_____
40. **STUDENT'S CONTRIBUTION FROM ASSETS**
    Take 20% of Line 39 .... $_____

Family Contribution

41. If one student is in college, add lines 24, 38, and 40. .... $_____
42. If two or more students are in college at the same time,
    add for each, Lines 25, 38, and 40. .... $_____

Notes to Appendices

[1] Contribution from student and parent assets will equal $0 if Parents' AGI (Line 1) is
   less than $50,000 and the parents are eligible to file a 1040A, 1040 EZ, or no tax
   return at all.

[2] Contribution from assets will equal $0 if student (and spouse) AGI (Line 1) is less
   than $50,000 and the student (and spouse) are eligible to file a 1040A or 1040EZ
   or no tax return at all.

■■■■■■■■■■■■■■■■■■■■■■■■■■■■■■■■■■■

INDEPENDENT STUDENTS WITH DEPENDENTS (2011/2012 ACADEMIC YEAR)

Contribution from Income (Student's and Spouse's)

1. Student's (and Spouse's) Adjusted Gross Income .... $____
2. Student's (and Spouse's) Tax-exempt Interest Income .... $____
3. Student's (and Spouse's) Veteran's Non-educational Benefits .... $____
4. Student's (and Spouse's) Other Untaxed Income and Benefits. This may include child support received,untaxed portions of pensions and IRA distributions, workers' compensation, disability payments, housing, food and living allowances for military, clergy or others .... $____
5. Deductible IRA, KEOGH, 403 (b) and 401(k) payments made by student (and spouse) .... $____
6. **Total Income.** Add Lines 1 through 5 .... $____
7. US Income Taxes paid .... $____
8. State Income Taxes paid .... $____
9. Social Security/Medicare Taxes paid .... $____
10. Child Support paid by you for another child .... $____
11. American Opportunity/Lifetime Learning credit, AmeriCorps awards, taxable earnings from Federal Work-Study (or other need-based work program) and other student financial aid that may have been included in Line 6. .... $____
12. Income Protection Allowance from Table A .... $____
13. Employment Expense Allowance. If both student and spouse work, enter 35% of the lower income or $3,500, whichever is less. If student qualifies as a single head of household, enter 35% of that income or $3,500, whichever is less. Otherwise, enter $0 .... $____
14. **Total Allowances.** Add Lines 7 through 13 .... $____
15. **Student's (and Spouse's) Available Income.** Line 6 minus Line 14 .... $____

Contribution from Assets (Student's and Spouse's)[2]

16. Cash, savings and checking accounts .... $____
17. Net Worth of real estate (excluding primary residence), investments, stocks, bonds, trusts, commodities, precious metals, college savings plans .... $____
18. Business and/or Commercial Farm Net Worth (excluding family farms and family-controlled small businesses) from Table B .... $____
19. **Total Assets.** Add Lines 16 through 18 .... $____
20. Asset Protection Allowance. From Table E .... $____
21. Discretionary Net Worth. Line 19 minus Line 20 .... $____
22. **CONTRIBUTION FROM ASSETS.** Multiply Line 21 by 7%. .... $____
23. Adjusted Available Income. Add Line 15 and Line 22. .... $____
24. **TOTAL CONTRIBUTION.** From Table D. If negative, enter 0. .... $____
25. Number in College Adjustment. Divide Line 24 by the number in college at least half-time at the same time. Quotient is the contribution/student ... $____

■■■■■■■■■■■■■■■■■■■■■■■■■■■■

INDEPENDENT STUDENTS WITHOUT DEPENDENTS (2011/2012 ACADEMIC YEAR)

Contribution from Income (Student's and Spouse's)

1. Student's (and Spouse's) Adjusted Gross Income .... $____
2. Student's (and Spouse's) Tax-exempt Interest Income .... $____
3. Student's (and Spouse's) Earned Income Credit .... $____
4. Student's (and Spouse's) Other Untaxed Income and Benefits. This may include child support received,untaxed portions of pensions and IRA distributions, workers' compensation, disability payments, housing, food and living allowances for military, clergy or others .... $____
5. Deductible IRA, KEOGH, 403 (b) and 401(k) payments made by student (and spouse) .... $____
6. **Total Income.** Add Lines 1 through 5 .... $____
7. US Income Taxes paid .... $____
8. State Income Taxes paid .... $____
9. Social Security/Medicare Taxes paid .... $____
10. Income Protection Allowance of $8,550 for single student or married student if spouse is also enrolled in college at least half time; $13,710 for married student if spouse is not enrolled at least half-time .... $____
11. Child Support paid by you for another child .... $____
11. American Opportunity/Lifetime Learning credit, AmeriCorps awards, taxable earnings from Federal Work-Study (or other need-based work program) and other student financial aid that may have been included in Line 6. .... $____
13. Employment Expense Allowance. If the student is single, enter $0. If the student is married and both the student and spouse are working, enter 35% of the lower income or $3,500, whichever is less. Otherwise, enter $0 .... $____
14. **Total Allowances.** Add Lines 7 through 13 .... $____
15. **Available Income.** Line 6 minus Line 14 .... $____
16. **Contribution from Income.** Take 50% of Line 15 .... $____

Contribution from Assets (Student's and Spouse's)[2]

17. Cash, savings and checking accounts .... $____
18. Net Worth of real estate (excluding primary residence), investments, stocks, bonds, trusts, commodities, precious metals, college savings plans .... $____
19. Business and/or Commercial Farm Net Worth (excluding family farms and family-controlled small businesses) from Table B .... $____
20. **Total Assets.** Add lines 17 through 19 .... $____
21. Asset Protection Allowance. From Table E .... $____
22. Discretionary Net Worth. Line 20 minus Line 21 .... $____
23. **CONTRIBUTION FROM ASSETS.** Multiply Line 22 by 20%. If negative, enter $0 .... $____
24. **TOTAL CONTRIBUTION.** Add Line 16 and Line 23 .... $____
25. Number in College Adjustment. Divide Line 24 by the number in college at least half-time at the same time. Quotient is the contribution/ student .. $____

Table A—Income Protection Allowance

Family Members (Incl. Student)	Dep. Student Allowance	Indep. Stdnt Allowance
2	$16,230	$21,660
3	$20,210	$26,960
4	$24,970	$33,300
5	$29,460	$39,300
6	$33,460	$45,950
Each Addit'l	$3,890	$5,180

Note: *For each student over one in college, subtract $2,760 from the appropriate maintenance allowance (for dependent students) or $3,690 from the appropriate maintenance allowance (for independent students).*

Table B—Adjustment of Business/Farm Net Worth

Net Worth of Business/Farm	Adjustment
To $115,000	40% of Net Worth
$115,001 to $345,000	$46,000, plus 50% of NW over $115,000
$345,001 to $580,000	$161,000, plus 60% of NW over $345,000
$580,501 or more	$302,000 plus 100% of NW over $580,000

Table C—Asset Protection Allowance, Dependent Student

Age of Older Parent	Two-Parent Family	One Parent Family
40-44	$39,900	$13,900
45-49	45,100	15,500
50-54	51,200	17,500
55-59	58,700	19,800
60-64	67,700	22,600
65 +	74,000	24,500

Table D—Parent and Independent Student Contribution

Adjusted Available Income (AAI)	Parent Contribution
To minus $3,409	-$750 (negative figure)
Minus $3,409 to plus $14,500	22% of AAI
$14,501 to $18,200	$3,190 plus 25% of AAI over $14,500
$18,201 to $21,900	$4,115 plus 29% of AAI over $18,200
$21,901 to $25,600	$5,188 plus 34% of AAI over $21,900
$25,601 to $29,300	$6,446 plus 40% of AAI over $25,600
$29,301 or more	$7,926 plus 47% of AAI over $29,300

Table E—Asset Protection Allowance, Independent Student

Age	Single	Married
25 & Under	$ 0	$ 0
26	900	2,500
29	3,500	10,200
32	6,200	17,800
35	8,900	25,500
38	11,500	33,100
45	14,900	42,900
50	16,700	48,800
65+	24,500	74,000

CALCULATIONS

••••••••••••••••••••••••••••••

College Planning Guides from Octameron

Don't Miss Out: The Ambitious Student's Guide to Financial Aid **$14.00**
    Hailed as the top consumer guide to student aid, Don't Miss Out covers scholarships, loans, and personal finance strategies. It will save readers hundreds, if not thousands of dollars in college costs.

The A's and B's of Academic Scholarships **$14.00**
    Money for being bright! This book describes 100,000 awards offered by nearly 1200 colleges. Best of all, most of these (which must be used at the sponsoring school) are not based on financial need.

Loans and Grants from Uncle Sam **$8.00**
    Increase your eligibility for federal student aid. This guide describes it all—the aid application process as well as loans and grants for students, parents and health professionals.

Financial Aid FinAncer: Expert Answers to College Financing Questions **$8.00**
    Learn how special family circumstances impact on student aid.

The Winning Edge: The Student-Athlete's Guide to College Sports **$9.00**
    It's all here. Scholarship opportunities. NCAA rules and regulations. Advice from coaches. Sample athletic resumes. Strategies, timetables, and worksheets—all to help you take your sport to college!

Behind the Scenes: An Inside Look at the College Admission Process **$8.00**
    Who get in, and why? Through question and answer sections and case studies, you can view the admission process from the inside. Originally written by Ed Wall, former Dean of Admission at Amherst College; updated by Janet Adams-Wall, Director of College Counseling at The Governor's Academy.

Do It Write: How to Prepare a Great College Application **$8.00**
    Personalize your essays so they stand out from the crowd. Author Gary Ripple is the former Admission Director at Lafayette College and the College of William and Mary

College Match: A Blueprint for Choosing the Best School for You **$12.00**
    Author Steve Antonoff combines dozens of easy-to-use worksheets with lots of practical advice to make sure you find schools that meet your needs and your preferences.

Campus Pursuit: Making the Most of the Visit and Interview **$7.00**
    Nervous about your interview? In his companion book to Do-It Write, Gary Ripple gives advice to help you shine, as well as show you how to maximize the benefits of a campus visit.

College.edu: On-Line Resources for the Cyber-Savvy Student **$12.00**
    Lost in Cyberspace? College.edu takes you to hundreds of useful sites on admission and financial aid, giving you Internet tips and warnings along the way.

Campus Daze: Easing the Transition from High School to College **$8.00**
    Learn what to expect during your first year of college and how to succeed starting on Day One. Author George Gibbs is the former Dean of Admission and Freshmen at Muhlenberg College.

College Majors That Work **$10.00**
    Get in. Get out. Get a job. Worksheets help match a student's goals and expectations with the right college major and explores how that choice plays out in the real world—influencing both career and lifestyle options. Written by Michael P. Viollt, President of Robert Morris College (IL).

Desk Set **$85.00**
    One copy of each of the above publications.

Ordering Information
    Send Orders to: Octameron Associates, PO Box 2748, Alexandria, VA 22301, or contact us at: 703-836-5480 (voice), 703-836-5650 (fax), octameron@aol.com (e-mail).

    Order Online: www.octameron.com.

    Postage and Handling: Please include $3.00 for one publication, $5.00 for two publications $6.00 for three publications and $7.00 for four or more publications (and for Desk Sets).

    Method of Payment: Payment must accompany order. We accept checks, money orders, American Express, Visa and MasterCard. If ordering by credit card, please include the card number and its expiration date.